EASTERN COACH WORKS

– A RETROSPECT –

ISBN 1 898432 51

Front Cover Illustration

Eastern National's distinctive FLF Lodekkas worked the express service from Southend to London's Victoria coach station and passengers were assured of a relaxed journey in the deep, red-upholstered seats with their comfortable headrests. At the rear of the lower saloon a partition divided the passengers from a large luggage area which had its own access through a centrally-located rear door. Thanks to the foresight of one of Eastern National's staff a full set of seats were carefully stored when the vehicles were eventually downgraded, being kept ready in the event that one day one might be purchased for restoration. The result can be seen when the vehicle appears at rallies and it is a credit to its proud owners who posed it at Bristol in 1994 for this photograph.

[Photo: John A. Senior

Produced for the Publishers
Venture Publications, Glossop Derbyshire,
by Mopok Graphics, Glossop SK13 8EH
using computerised origination

EASTERN COACH WORKS

– A RETROSPECT –

by

Duncan Roberts

&

John Senior

Venture *publications*

CONTENTS

FOREWORD

The Coach Factory at Lowestoft was a local institution with nationwide connections. Built on the site of its original owner's bus operating base it achieved an enviable reputation – well earned and thoroughly deserved – for the quality of its workmanship.

During the sixty-five years or so that bus bodies were built on the site, first for the United company who originally owned the factory, later for operators throughout the great Tilling group, and later still for customers throughout the United Kingdom and as far away as America and Hong Kong, Greece and Saudi Arabia, Baghdad and China it provided employment for generations of craftsman, many of whom followed their fathers and grandfathers before them.

Indeed one of the most striking aspects of the factory workforce story is this family connection, with fathers and sons, brothers, cousins, uncles and every possible combination of relatives working busily under one roof – truly a family concern on a great scale.

The changes in modes of transport during the life of the coachworks were legion. Great liners crossed the oceans, aeroplanes were developed to fly faster than sound, railway trains were built to travel over 200 mph. Men flew to the moon, and walked on it. The channel tunnel was begun. But throughout all these changes life in Laundry Lane, later Eastern Way, seemed to have a steady purpose largely unaffected by events elsewhere. Even a world war couldn't completely stop the factory. The traditional bus, be it ever so humble, seemed set to leave the Lowestoft factory as regularly as the tide brought the trawlers back.

Sadly the sure foundation was gradually being eroded. Many of the signs were buried deep in board meetings held hundreds of miles from Lowestoft; others were hidden in deals – 'stitched up' as the modern idiom has it – which had everything to do with Politics but often little to do with people's jobs in East Anglia.

The enormous changes in the bus industry over the last two decades are sufficient to fill a book in themselves – indeed this publisher has already produced one such volume which is referred to in later pages. Whether ECW might have survived had it been free of political interference, outside interests and, perhaps, bloody mindedness is for the reader to judge. Or was the industry just unable to sustain it in recession?

A great debt of gratitude is owed to all those people who have searched their souls and opened their hearts to talk for hours about life at the coach factory. Those interviews, fascinating and demonstrating the pride and loyalty which existed, provided much of the information upon which the first half of this book is based. It became a labour of love, such was the enthusiasm they evinced. I hope you will feel I have done justice to you all, and to your factory.

John A. Senior
Glossop
July 1995

INTRODUCTION

The Coach Factory at Lowestoft was both a supplier of quality bus and coach bodywork to the nation as well as a key local employer. Today we live in very materialistic times and for the most part people derive their living from an employer who is compartmentalised into a segment, albeit major, of Monday through Friday. Fifty years ago people looked to their employer for the basis of their social life as well. As the 'seventies dawned this diminished but at Lowestoft the trend was bucked and even now a thriving ECW Retired (and former) Employees Association meets weekly in the town.

This gives us an essential clue to the ethos of the plant on Eastern Way.

My own memories of the coach factory go back almost to the cradle, as the company who bodied the buses of Crosville. But even then the most striking memory is when I was in my early teens, on holiday in East Anglia for the first time, I managed to persuade my parents to 'phone ECW to see if I could "look round". Today as the Managing Director of a very busy company, such a thing would be a complete anathema, yet Len Webb the Labour Officer not only said "yes" but personally gave us a guided tour of over three hours. Such as the pride in the business and the family atmosphere that this was not even remotely a burden to him.

Sadly the coach factory fell foul of the dubious policies of the Conservative Government of Margaret Thatcher, as well as a mortal blow from within the organised Labour movement. The plant is now a memory, the products will certainly be with us for many years to come – unless the Eurocrats or more likely our own disabled lobby push the UK bus industry to yet another unwarranted precipice with unwarranted demands for nigh *universal* access. The spirit lives on and Len Webb, the secretary of the Employees Association still has a substantial membership who carry on the tradition of the plant. At eighty years of age he still reflects the pride evident in 1966.

This book builds on the 'nuts and bolts' of the history so ably put together by Alan Townsin and Maurice Doggett. Hopefully John Senior and I have captured both the style of the product as well as some of the more unusual offerings but, more importantly, we have sought to capture the human aspect before the mists of time finally shroud all but distant memory. Innovation was the keyword and, as an operator today, I find it saddening that the coach factory's former competitors today beseech us to buy 'allow bodies etc' as some revelation, yet it is one they utterly ignored during the easy time but one which ECW treated as the mundane.

This book is dedicated to the Lowestoft Coachbuilder – we will certainly never see his like again: We are the poorer.

Duncan Roberts
Sheffield
June 1995

PHOTOCREDITS

Once again the publishers have been fortunate in being able to draw on a wide variety of material to illustrate this book, and acknowledge the assistance of those who have provided this material. The principal sources, as in previous volumes in this series, have been the photographs gathered together from Eastern Coach Works by various members of the company's management and staff and passed for safe keeping into the Senior Transport Archive, along with those taken by the Company's official photographers over the years but loaned to the publisher by individuals. Additionally, material from the Leyland archives, also passed to the Senior Transport Archive when research into that company was being undertaken in the 1980s, has been used.

More recently ECW's last official photographer, Brian Ollington of Gorleston, has been most helpful in providing prints to our requirements from information passed to us by Maurice Doggett, co-Author of the earlier volumes in the series, who catalogued the negatives for Ollington's some years ago. The copyright in some of the earlier official views now rests with SJ Butler who kindly agreed to the illustrations being used.

Other contributors who have provided material include:-

Maurice Doggett; Roy Marshall; Geoff Atkins; Alan Townsin; Duncan Roberts; Dennis Mitchell; Mrs Iris Wright; The Lowestoft Journal; Gerald Vincent; Brian Ratcliffe; Len Webb; John Senior; and Arnold Richardson of Photobus. The cover illustration of the Eastern National Lodekka was taken at the Bristol Rally in 1994 by John Senior who thanks the owners for their assistance in setting up this view. If anyone has inadvertently been omitted from this list we offer our apologies.

ACKNOWLEDGEMENTS

The research necessary for the production of this book has been conducted over the last twenty-five years. During that time John Senior, co-author, has researched and published histories of many of the companies with whom ECW was or later became associated, particularly those in the one-time Leyland empire, or with whom it competed. Interviews with the Directors and top management of ACV, Park Royal Vehicles Ltd, Chas H Roe Ltd, Leyland Truck & Bus and later Leyland Vehicles Ltd, Duple, Plaxtons, Leyland National, NBC and Volvo gave an unrivalled opportunity to assess the strengths and weaknesses of products and factories and to compare what was happening in those factories with what ECW were doing. The open and frank responses to questions, accompanied by the opportunities to look round the factories – often unaccompanied and with camera, video or other recording equipment – and to talk directly to men on the shop floor were not wasted. Some of the video interviews will one day make a most interesting record of those people's achievements.

In 1976 came the long-awaited invitation to visit ECW at Lowestoft and to discuss with the newly-installed Plant Director, John Bloor, the possibility of publishing a series of books on the company. John took a friendly and very great interest in the project and introduced me to many of his workforce, personally endorsing the value of the project to them as a means of promoting their company. Those contacts later blossomed and, after closure, a further round of interviews took place in the Rockcliffe Hotel and at the homes of many former employees.

Trevor Westgate of the local newspaper, The Lowestoft Journal, was also must supportive and gave great encouragement as have Jarrolds and other local shops. The value of a record of the company's achievements and place in Lowestoft's history was recognised and their help with promotion was invaluable.

Alan Townsin and Maurice Doggett, co-authors of the previous three volumes have assisted with this volume and also checked some of the detail though the responsibility for any errors must lay with my co-author Duncan Roberts and myself in this volume.

The assistance of the Comptroller of Her Majesty's Stationery Office in providing copies of the six patents from which the brief details were extracted and included in one of the Appendices is also acknowledged with thanks.

The late Sid Wright, former Works Manager, and his wife Iris were particularly kind and helpful, providing the means of meeting people who might otherwise have slipped through the net. Sid's neighbour Stan George, former Chief Designer, was most helpful and cleared up many mysteries. Stan, perhaps, typified the attitude of everyone who became involved; where I had expected a measure of bitterness at what had happened there was instead a much stronger pride in what had been achieved and still, after retirement, loyalty to the 'family business' as it surely was in so many ways.

Interviewing these various people was fascinating, I could have carried on for months! Unfortunately commercial constraints eventually decree that a line has to be drawn somewhere but I sincerely hope that all who assisted will be pleased with the outcome, that those who were not given the opportunity will understand the reasons, and that anyone who helped but whose name has been missed will accept my sincere apologies.

The names are recorded in strict alphabetical order since it would not be fair to single out any one individual when so much help has been given by so many.

Colin Bailey; Ron Bennett; Lord Black; John Bloor; David Burnicle; SJ Butler; Mick Carolan; Bernie Carr; Ron Clarke; George Crisp; Maurice Doggett; Jack Field: John Foster; Lawrence Gall; Norman George; Stan George; Sandy Glennie; Gordon Goodman; Gus Halkes; Ron Hall; Alan Hunton; Doug Jack; Alan Lark; Dennis Mitchell; Philip and Audrey Morton; Brian Ratcliffe; Russel Richardson; Mrs CH Roe; Bill Shirley; John Simmons; Bob Smith; Rodney Swarbrick; Alan Townsin; Gerald Vincent; Len Webb; Trevor Westgate; Brian Wright; Sid and Iris Wright.

FRONTISPIECE

One

At the turn of the century Lowestoft was still a genteel town dependent on fishing, farming and benefitting from the visitors who came to enjoy a holiday by the seaside. The Great Eastern Railway's smart blue locomotives brought the visitors into the town's railway station and from 1904 the same company's buses were ready to take them to their final destination.

Lowestoft also had its own municipal transport undertaking, of course, and its narrow-gauge double-decked trams ran from the Pakefield terminus along London Road before rumbling across the swing bridge, through the town and out along the Yarmouth Road to the terminus at Lowestoft North Station.

The Great Eastern buses were garaged and maintained at premises in Denmark Road and these premises were to form the birthplace of what would, in later years, become Eastern Coach Works. The choice of Lowestoft as the home for the coach factory was quite simply determined by the fact that an Edwardian entrepreneur, E. B. Hutchinson, saw opportunities to develop a viable bus network when the Great Eastern Railway decided to pull out of the town in January 1913.

Hutchinson's new venture was curtailed by the outbreak of war and the compulsory requisitioning of many of his buses, to be sent to aid the war effort in northern France. Undaunted, he pressed on, and converted many of the remainder to operate on town gas or paraffin. Hutchinson was a live wire and his enthusiasm for his work led him to seek the means of extending his fleet as soon as the war was over – a time when buses were not easy to acquire.

Like many others he was well aware of the potential for exploiting the motor vehicles which had proved their worth in the terrible wartime conditions. The whole perception of the internal combustion engine had changed as men had seen what it could achieve, and a generation of ex-servicemen would start to create bus companies throughout the land.

Hutchinson had created a company – United Automobile Services – with enormous potential and a vast territory. Starting in East Anglia he worked his way northwards to County Durham and also had connections with Underwoods, who ran in Sheffield, Nottinghamshire and Derbyshire. The rapid growth of his empire created a need for large numbers of buses and, like many others, he had to resort to the purchase and overhaul of ex-military chassis which the government was offering for sale. His astuteness also led him to organise the location, purchase,

Ernest Boyd Hutchinson in later years.

A sylvan scene in Edwardian Lowestoft. A solitary tramcar makes its way down the street in between the horse-drawn carts making their deliveries.

Above: Lorry buses were built on AEC Y-type chassis, some being conversions of an ambulance-type construction which the military had used in the 1914-18 war. Although the end product was fairly crude, it allowed operators such as United to get started with the peacetime business of providing transport at the earliest opportunity.

Below: An extract from a brochure produced by United to promote its products at the 1921 Commercial Motor Show in London.

═══FOREWORD.═══

NEVER has there been a more specialized Industry than Motor 'Bus Body Building

In this industry, demanding the highest degree of skill in execution and forethought in production. "UNITED" Bodies stand paramount, the reason being that, guided by the experience gained in building Bodies for their own large fleet of Public Service vehicles, the Company have discovered the very essentials necessary to combine the two most desirable features, viz., Rigidity and Strength with Lightness in body construction.

Experience plays the largest part in production and the United Automobile Services, Ltd. now offer the finest workmanship based on 18 years experience : Ample proof that their craftsmanship has been highly esteemed lies in the fact that 70% repeat orders have been received during the last twelve months.

As masters of 'Bus Body construction, "UNITED" have been favoured with orders from all parts of the world and from many of the foremost Transport Companies

The "UNITED" Factory is equipped with the most modern plant, and up-to-date methods are operative.

A thorough study has been made of the recommendations of the Ministry of Transport, and careful attention has been given to their projected requirements in the construction of light bodies for 'buses.

No work is too difficult or complicated, and with utmost confidence in our ability to completely satisfy our customers, we solicit your enquiries, which will receive expeditious and minute attention.

recovery and then subsequent shipment back to Lowestoft of vehicles abandoned on the battlefields of France and Belgium which had not been recovered by the official 'clean-up' squads after hostilities ended.

It was this policy of reconditioning and modifying chassis to be used in his own very successful and constantly expanding fleet which provided the expertise Eastern Coach Works was able to draw upon in later years. The understanding of an operator's needs, and the knowledge that the success of a bus body was its ability to meet those needs, was never forgotten in Eastern Way (as it later became).

In 1919 EBH (as Hutchinson was always known) purchased land in Laundry Lane to allow for expansion of the maintenance facilities needed for the growing United fleet. This facility was soon extended to allow space for the reconditioning of rudimentary wartime lorry/bus bodywork, and, very soon, the building of completely new bus bodies. Chassis were completely reconditioned and often substantially modified by being lengthened or converted to forward-control.

The bodybuilding and engineering sides of the business were kept separate and in 1920, shortly after the move to Laundry Lane, the first bodybuilding apprentice, Albert Goate, was taken on at the age of 14 and straight from school. He served a seven year apprenticeship followed by one year as a journeyman, those being the normal arrangements of the time and ensuring that full money was paid only after workers reached the age of 21. His foreman was Ted Godwin and he later recalled that with shipbuilding then going through a bad time quite a number of shipwrights joined the company.

This combination of operator/manufacturer was almost certainly unique on this scale, but without doubt the very special expertise introduced by the shipwrights must also have stood the company in good stead. A skilled understanding of the correct and appropriate use of different timbers and the eye for good design which forms such a basic part of nautical affairs would very shortly put EBH's company at the forefront of the industry.

Such was the rate of its development that by 1921 United was exhibiting at the Commercial Motor Show in London. It was offering its Norfolk body, designed by Mr Heard the manager, and as can be seen from the advertisement, the bus was designed for one-man-operation.

By 1922 United had become a very significant employer in the town. It was employing 300 people, operating the buses, repairing, reconditioning and also constructing

A cheerful group photographed outside the factory in 1922. The open-top bus in the background registered WR 6170 is interesting. According to PSV Circle records it is an AEC Y-type wartime subsidy chassis from the United fleet carrying what may well be an ex-London General B-type body. The WR registration is thought to relate to the Underwood's operation with which United was associated. It would almost certainly be at Lowestoft for refurbishment.

United adopted the practice of naming its early model types and its first, the Norfolk, was a 24-to-26-seat lightweight design, seen here in an advertisement for the 1921 Commercial Motor Show. United claimed to be the first operator to use pneumatic tyres on a vehicle classed as a 'heavy motor car'. This break-through had been achieved by joint collaboration between United, Daimler and Goodyear. Note the stylised logo with the large letter U and the two addresses – Lowestoft and Bishop Auckland.

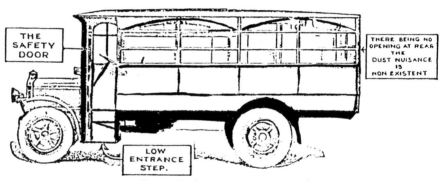

The Cromer body was a medium-size coach shown here mounted on a Star chassis made by the Star Motor Co Ltd of Wolverhampton for whom United was an agent; this was one of several agencies held.

The half canopy design, seen here on an AEC 415 chassis, would find favour again in the mid-'thirties with North Western and Crosville, amongst others, and on Leyland, Bristol and Tilling Stevens chassis. The United logo was as used on the Company's letterheads and publicity, and a similar style was adopted for the logo on the vehicles of the associated Underwood concern. United's vehicles were finished in a yellow and brown livery and this was one of 90 generally similar vehicles.

new bodies at the rate of around two per week. The bodybuilding operation was kept separate and 'In-house' requirements alone would have kept the craftsmen busy for United was putting vehicles into service in batches as large as 100 at a time, but there was also a steady flow of orders from 'outside' customers.

The company was now becoming very important to the local economy, having become a thriving and expanding concern with steadily increasing employment opportunities. The jobs on offer would be more attractive to most men than working on the land or on the trawlers, and, from all accounts, probably better paid. In line with these trends by the end of 1925 further extensions to the factory were required to meet demand. Several of the men who joined the company in the 'twenties were able to assist in recording the history when work started on this publishing project in the mid-'eighties and most had memories of hard work but good team spirit and the satisfaction of work well done.

The first recorded involvement with the design department of Lancashire bus and lorry builder Leyland Motors occurred in 1928 when the Lowestoft craftsmen built some charabanc bodywork to Leyland design, using Leyland drawings, on bonnetted Leyland Lioness chassis. This was at a time when the Lancashire company was unable to meet the demand for its bodies and farmed some contracts out. The work was clearly satisfactory for further such contracts were placed later that year, again using Leyland drawings, but this time on the forward-control Lion PLSC chassis.

The scale of United's operation was starting to cause alarm within the railway companies, as was that of other large companies such as Crosville, based in Chester, and already a customer of the coach factory. The railways were seeking to reduce losses in rural areas by curtailing the activities of these bus operators, intending instead to operate their own bus services. Accordingly, in June 1929, United was approached by the LNER with a view to a takeover. Before any decision could be made another offer was received. This was from The Tilling and British Electric Traction companies group, TBAT (Tilling and British Automobile Traction), which wanted to acquire United to allow it to extend and develop its existing bus operations. The upshot was the sale of the company in July 1929, jointly to the LNER and TBAT, and the resignation of EBH.

He sent a personal letter to his employees recording his great sorrow at the turn of events and thanking them most sincerely for their loyalty and hard work. Lest there be any misunderstanding it should be remembered that there was a very real danger that the railway companies might, in 1930, have been given powers to acquire these territorial bus companies compulsorily and EBH clearly had little choice but to sell when he did. United's new manager was HP Stokes, from Plymouth Corporation Transport Department, probably better known as father of Donald, later Lord Stokes, Leyland's ace bus salesman.

Crosland Taylor, writing in the history of the Crosville concern, recalled that after the LMS purchased Crosville in 1929 there was a breathing space while they took stock and wondered what to do with it. Doubtless the situation was similar with United's new owners.

The factory continued under the supervision of Messrs Romer and Cladish, both of whom played an important part in shaping the growing company's fortunes. A new employee at this time was one Lennie Webb, engaged by Works Superintendent Alfred Cladish as a fourteen-year-old in the fitters shop. With occasional periods away Len was to serve in the factory until 1981, a proud record and a diverse career as will be seen. He recalls his early days as being spent doing hard and dirty work – the fitting shop had an earth and cinder floor – and much of his time was spent

Above: A larger, heavyweight coach built on a Gilford chassis is shown here. Gilford was growing in importance in 1929 and had also been set up to recondition ex-military vehicles for resale, in this case of American origin.

Centre: The AJS coach illustrated below has an old-fashioned appearance created largely by the set-back radiator. A J Stevens Ltd was another Wolverhampton-based company which built motor cycles, cars and light coach chassis. The company went into liquidation in 1931.

Foot: Leyland Motors of Lancashire produced a rather splendid six-cylinder normal-control chassis in 1929, designated the Lioness LTB1. It had also developed an all-weather body with roll-back canvas top. Such was the pressure on the Lancashire company's bodybuilding facility due to the success of its new model range that other companies built Leyland-style bodies under contract. This example was built by United to Leyland drawings and The Crosville Motor Company was one customer for this product.

Left: This express single-decker was operated by East Midland Motor Services Ltd, successor to Underwoods, and is shown here lettered for a service from Nottingham to Yarmouth. It was photographed in 1929 by G H F Atkins, a then youthful bus enthusiast who still provides photographs for Venture Publications and others.

Below: A rear view showing how the smooth lines and neat styling had evolved by the early 'thirties. This is another example on a Gilford chassis.

worked on the bathing huts south of Clarence Pier. The seaside environment helped many men to find such employment and continuity of employment would no doubt be given to the family men. Even the 'old-timers' were not immune from this treatment yet each autumn they would go back to Laundry Lane and expect to be taken on again.

as striker for the blacksmith with whom he worked. Much time was also spent polishing stainless trim for coaches on the buffing machines.

After a year he was laid off, with many others, and was away from the factory for some 4-5 months. When he returned he was able to go into the panel shop where he was introduced to the band saw – a tool he would use throughout his career until he moved off the shop floor. He recalls that lay-offs were an accepted fact of life and that there was no rancour or embarrassment, one day you had a job and the next you didn't. The depression was making life very difficult and he also recalls Romer calling everyone together, some 80 or so employees in the coachbuilding plant at that time, to announce that wages were to be reduced by one penny an hour (an 8-10% reduction depending on grade) and that overtime would in future be paid only at normal rates. This would be around 1932.

May was the time for the big lay-offs, when the new season's orders had been completed, and the opportunity was taken to get rid of all the tradesmen who had been employed just for the winter rush. Webb was a bronze medal life-saver and worked at the Lowestoft swimming pool near Sparrow's Nest one year. Another year he

The important TBAT connection gave access to many new customers 'within the group' and an early portent was the arrival of one of Midland Red's antediluvian looking S-type SOS vehicles to be rebodied by United. This was the first Lowestoft contract for the group and following the successful completion of the first body 82 further vehicles were so treated. These were allocated to several TBAT companies including Trent, Llandudno Coaching Company, and Ortona in addition to the main Midland Red fleet.

Feeling that things were looking up perhaps, United patented a sunshine roof in 1930 and fitted it to 50 bodies for its own fleet. There was now considerable variety in customers and chassis types passing through the coach factory but the TBAT connection would soon ensure that more and more business would go to the big companies. Municipal work continued, however, and four Guy saloons were delivered 'down the road' to the local operator, Lowestoft Corporation.

By 1931 TBAT had digested the situation and a wholesale rationalisation of bus services in East Anglia was introduced. United was operating in every county along the east coast of England from Suffolk to

Northumberland but the new arrangements saw Lincolnshire Road Car taking over services in Lincolnshire from New Year's Day 1931 whilst on 14th July that same year Eastern Counties Omnibus Company Limited was incorporated to take over the services in Norfolk and north Suffolk, in addition to those of TBAT companies Eastern Counties Road Car of Ipswich, Ortona of Cambridge and the Peterborough Electric Traction Co Ltd.

This move allowed United to concentrate on its northern area but meant that the coach factory passed to Eastern Counties' control with effect from July 1931. A Tilling man, J F. Heaton, Chairman of Thomas Tilling Ltd, became Chairman of both United and Eastern Counties whilst Joseph Worssam, Manager of Eastern Counties, now became responsible *inter alia* for matters in the coach building company in addition to the operating fleet.

One of the last batches of buses to be built by United was for Lowestoft Corporation although the one shown, the last of eight, was actually delivered after the factory had changed ownership. The design was unusual for the coach factory, having echoes of London features, particularly the straight staircase. The half-drop windows in the rear bays were also unusual. Subsequent orders for the local operator went to Massey of Wigan so perhaps all was not quite satisfactory with the contract.

Leyland Motors were sufficiently interested in United's sunshine body on the Tiger TS3 chassis to arrange for it to be photographed at the usual location for its own official photographs near to the Lancashire factory.

Almost immediately after the change of financial control the Birmingham & Midland Motor Omnibus Co Ltd, a major TBAT constituent, sent one of its four-year-old SOS S-type vehicles to Lowestoft for a rebodying exercise, seen after completion below. Such was the rate of development of bus design that the original four-year-old body was already obsolescent. The operator had stripped out all the reusable components before despatching the vehicle to Lowestoft.

Two

Eastern Counties in charge 1931-1936

When Eastern Counties was incorporated by TBAT to take charge of the operation of bus and coach services in East Anglia it could be excused for perhaps finding the thriving coach factory which it also inherited a little outside its normal remit as a bus operating company.

Indications are that it left well alone. Arnold J Romer was appointed to the position of Works Manager and he and Alfred Cladish and their team continued with the good work. Romer had been with Thornycroft before moving to Midland Red. Both organisations were chassis manufacturers, and this experience was put to good use whilst he was at Lowestoft.

This continually recurring theme of a coach builder with chassis manufacturing and engineering experience explains why, in later years, people at Lowestoft could rightly feel that the men from Lancashire were the ones who were out-of-touch. Few at Leyland were able to grasp the fact that there was experience in that remote factory going back 50 years before the bright young men from Lancashire stuck their oars in, and Lowestoft had what Leyland never had had, operating experience.

They felt that if only someone at Leyland had had the wit to see what was on offer from Bristol and Lowestoft, as an entity, things could have been very different for Leyland, let alone the other two. But we anticipate our story and the (much) later misfortunes brought about by mergers, mediocrity and meddlers.

After boldly emblazoning the new company's name above the doors fronting onto Laundry Lane one of the first jobs was to repaint a varied and somewhat motley selection of buses from the new parent company – Eastern Counties had acquired 534 vehicles on 19 chassis makes. Copious quantities of Foo Chow Red paint for the new colour scheme arrived and the painters got cracking. Perhaps that was when the singing began in the paint shops though one wonders what was happening elsewhere in the factory at the time.

The economic situation was improving and the factory was growing as more business was obtained. Fewer people were laid off and the pattern of employment became steadier. A new panel shop was constructed to cope with the growing demand and the girls in the trimmers shop, working on upholstery and interior trim, were moved down from their previous balcony location.

Soon the major orders came and one of the first was from the West Yorkshire Road Car Company of Harrogate, a customer whose name would appear regularly in the order books over the coming years. The new Group status helped to gain orders and output began to rise steadily, from just over 200 bodies in 1932 to 358 in 1934. It was not all plain sailing, however, and in between bouts of frenzied activity there were still some layoffs when work ran out. The easing of the depression helped and production had leapt to 526 vehicles per year by 1935.

The benefit of membership of the TBAT Group was now very apparent – orders were coming in steadily from many of the companies within the group who had not previously been customers of the factory, in addition to BET members buying through the British Electrical Federation. A new policy of involving customers in matters concerning the design and finish of vehicles was instituted by Romer who recognised that the earlier one-major-customer situation had probably stifled many innovative ideas. He now attended half-yearly board meetings at Tilling's London headquarters where the directors were able to review these and other matters. Advertising seems to have been minimal in this period and it may be that there was as much work available as could be handled at some times of the year when looking at the production figures

THE

"EASTERN COUNTIES"

WAY

is the

"UNITED"

WAY

between

NEWCASTLE

DARLINGTON

LEEDS

DONCASTER

LINCOLN

NORWICH

GT. YARMOUTH

&

LOWESTOFT

An extract from a 1932 Eastern Counties time-table leaving no doubt in passengers' minds that ECOC was United's successor in the area.

above. Creating an even balance was clearly what was required.

Amongst the big names now regularly placing orders were Crosville, Eastern Counties themselves, Eastern National, Hants & Dorset, Hebble, North Western, East Yorkshire, West Yorkshire and United. There had been some municipal orders, including a batch of the factory's first double-deckers, on AEC Regents for Great Yarmouth, and a batch of similar vehicles for Lowestoft when its trams were abandoned in May 1931, but the main business was from the companies. Lowestoft did not buy any more new buses until 1945, and they were not bodied by ECOC or its successor, so even the local operator could not be relied upon to keep its small orders coming into the factory.

Double-deckers were very much in the minority in those years, reflecting the nature of business carried out by the majority of the coach factory's customers. Similarly the chassis tended to be of AEC, Bristol, Dennis, Leyland or Tilling-Stevens manufacture. Some of the smaller manufacturers popular in the 'twenties had gone out of business, others were not being operated by the bigger undertakings.

Although the figures show a rising trend they do not reveal the pattern which those working in the factory knew only too well. Len Webb and Gus Halkes, two names familiar to generations of coach works' employees, recalled over 60 years later that as in any factory which was involved in building coaches they would experience seasonal fluctuations. Vehicles were wanted for the beginning of the season and most operators would order no more until they saw the end of season results, causing the lay-offs until the next orders came in during the autumn.

Gus had spent some time at Claytons in Lincoln in the mid-'twenties, working on Pullman carriages, vehicles finished to a very high standard indeed, and recalls his starting rate at ECOC being 1/3½d per hour for a skilled man.

Len Webb also remarked that the foundations for the family atmosphere had already been established by this time. The coach factory was, by and large, a good place to work when there was work. A pattern emerged of jobs for the boys, but in a far more acceptable and literal manner than this expression usually implies! In a far-sighted policy it became the practice to encourage youngsters to join their fathers or uncles, subject always to suitability (of both generations), and right to the very end of the coach works' existence people could look back to two or three generations of family involvement.

It was claimed by management that this approach meant that work in some ways became a family affair and that family loyalties would help smooth over difficulties. One can imagine examples of clans at war in some areas but perhaps the East Anglians are more suited to this way of working – certainly it was still the norm to the end of apprenticeships in the factory. The employment of twins must have made life interesting, Teddy Gamble and his brother had started with United even before Len Webb's time and Sid Wright recalled several other instances whilst he was helping with his reminiscences, including two of the four Mitchells who worked in the factory.

Eastern Counties were not alone in experiencing the seasonal fluctuation, similar tales emanate from Plaxton,

The original swing bridge, seen below, was a familiar landmark for many years. The bus is a Leyland bodied Leyland Titan. Once Eastern Counties became owner of the coachworks most of its bodies were built in Lowestoft. The building in the background is the one-time famous pier pavilion, seen above in more leisurely days.

Buses built in Lowestoft were purchased and operated by customers far and wide, as here. Caledonian operated in Scotland from Dumfries whilst, at the other extreme, Western National operated in rural south west England. The vehicles shown in both illustrations are built on Dennis chassis, above being seen a Federation-style body whilst the line outside the old frontage are of the small Ace model, known to one-and-all as the Flying Pig.

Harrington, Burlingham, Duple, Park Royal and so on. There was another common thread in that the first three organisations mentioned were in seaside towns where casual labour would be required 'just for the season' and this helped those temporarily laid off from their proper job.

What began to save the day, however, was a substantial business in rebodying older chassis, almost a repeat of the earliest days. Crosville and North Western were just two examples of fleets where major renewals took place and there was a steady and very substantial stream of chassis coming from Chester and Stockport. On a smaller scale ten bodies were built to Midland Red design on SOS chassis in 1932 but gradually the Federation business tailed off since ECOC was building for long life and BET, as always, was looking for lower-cost less-durable products.

One notable feature was the ability and willingness to adapt bodies to operator's requirements, this being easier when the large volume in-house orders for United were less prevalent. This adaptability became a very important feature of Lowestoft production and some very clever modifications took place to give customer's vehicles an individual appearance without significant additional cost. Leo Page looked after engineering, and also organised the bowls matches between departments or with ECOC's road staff.

One feature which North Western championed from the mid-'thirties was the half canopy layout, yet this had been incorporated in United designs of the 'twenties as shown on page 14. Some would say there's nothing new under the sun.

Reflecting the increase in business on offer, extensions to the factory were opened in March 1933, November 1933 and late 1934. Another well-known name appeared on the payroll at this time when Bill Shirley took up a position as foreman in the coach-fitting shop in 1934. He came from Weymanns at Addlestone, having previously been at Metro-Cammell Carriage and Wagon Co in Birmingham. In both cases he had been involved in the company's first all-metal bus body assembly.

Whilst at Met-Cam he had worked with Colin Bailey, who went to Leyland after being head-hunted by Henry Spurrier in 1935 to sort out the problems of corrosion and weak framing in the V-front Leyland metal-framed bodies. Shirley moved to Leyland Motors that same year, 1935, as body assembly shop foreman. Clearly a man who was going places he was equally clearly in all the right places at the right times to see the advantages and disadvantages of metal-framing in an industry still firmly wedded to timber construction. He was ahead of his time at Lowestoft but his day would come as we shall see.

Two youngsters who were taken on by Alf Cladish in 1935 were Stan George and Sid Wright, Stan in the drawing office and Sid first as the Chief Inspector Basil Terry's lad, a 'progressor', and later with the setters out. Basil organised the weekly factory sweepstake and the young Sid took the tickets round on a Saturday morning, a useful way of getting to know the factory and the people who worked in it. The Chief Inspector was also active in many other areas of the factory's leisure activity.

Orders continued to increase in size and frequency, and to keep pace with the need for space the original garage was demolished in 1935 (though the underground fuel tank remained, causing some perplexion after closure in 1987 when hardly anyone knew what it was or why it was there) and alterations to the offices took place. Two storage sheds were also erected in the first half of 1936.

The workforce had now risen to 950 and was producing, on average, one double-deck and nine single-deckers each week. It was decided by the Group Directors that it was time to let the company stand on its own feet, and also to allow a change of name to make it easier to look for municipal business in order to try to keep the order books full and even out the imbalance which still frequently necessitated lay-offs. Whilst this was happening A J Romer – 'the old man' to one-and-all – who had managed the operation of the factory so successfully since 1928, was offered promotion to another position within the Tilling organisation, at Bristol's manufacturing plant at Brislington. A popular boss, he was given a marvellous send-off on Saturday 16th May, 1936, when a good meal with plenty of beer in the canteen was rounded off with an evening's entertainment from members of the various shops.

Bill Bramham met his new workforce that evening and must have been impressed by the comradeship and spirit of togetherness. He took over the reins on the Monday morning, and soon afterwards a new company – entitled Eastern Coach Works – was formed.

All buses have to be tested for stability to ensure that they will not easily tip over in an accident and here one of Western National's Aces undergoes the tilt-test. In the background a Crosville double-decker nears completion.

Crosville sent large numbers of its old vehicles to rebodied at Lowestoft, those in the illustration above being Leyland Lions of 1926-29 vintage which were rebodied in batches in 1933 and then in 1935-36. The shallow windows give a clue as to the high floor level on these rebodied chassis but the vehicles looked very smart when completed. Another customer which would later indulge in wholesale rebodying of old Tilling Stevens chassis was North Western Road Car, but this handsome coach is on a Leyland Tiger chassis. The Stockport based company switched from its previous body suppliers, Leyland, Brush and Tilling, and placed most of its orders with Lowestoft once it had assessed the performance of this batch of 25 vehicles, delivered in 1932. It continued to purchase some luxury coaches from Harrington, of Hove, but this was perhaps as much for dual-sourcing as for any other reason. Certainly NWRC was a major customer for ECOC and ECW until Nationalisation prevented it purchasing any further examples.

Three
Eastern Coach Works is founded, July 1936

The man appointed by the Tilling Group to be its new broom was to create a northern link which continued unbroken for 40 years, for he was a Yorkshireman. William (Bill) Bramham was appointed to the new position of General Manager and brought with him a wealth of experience.

He had been at the Yorkshire coachbuilder Charles H Roe of Crossgates, Leeds, since 1926 and in his ten years had risen to a senior position with many contacts throughout the industry. Roe was a traditional bodybuilder, famed for the strength and quality of its teak-framed bodies, and also a major supplier to many municipal customers.

He came to Lowestoft a few weeks before ECW's formation and brought with him Roe's chief estimator, Ralph Sugden, though the latter had to be content initially with a position as assistant stores officer. Sugden had been at Roe's factory since 1924 and the loss of the two senior men was a bitter blow as Mrs Roe recalled when interviewed many years later. Sugden soon rose to become ECW's Commercial Manager and Deputy General Manager. Alfred Cladish now became Works Manager, continuing to work his way up through the coach factory management.

Bramham continued to develop the business along the lines established by the previous regime, though the notice which appeared alongside the clocking points warning of severe penalties for wrongful clocking in and out soon after his arrival suggested that he saw some things had been getting a bit sloppy. Alongside was another notice informing of the change of company name. Since there were no such things as Contracts of Employment, and no sick pay, pension or holiday pay, shop floor workers were largely unaffected by the change.

Len Webb recalls one change which did cause some concern – the loss of concessionary tickets on the Eastern Counties bus network. The practice had been to allocate two free tickets for travel to any point on the system to each employee each year, the one-and-only perk it seems. Even this disappeared under the new ownership.

Working conditions and practices remained much as they had been. The batch system of manufacturing components continued, there being normally thirty vehicles to each batch with all manufacturing being arranged to produce sufficient items for the thirty vehicles in question. In the bodyshops gangs of three or four worked on the

BUILT TO ENDURE

10 Years old

Long Life Between January and May 1937, 48 E.C.W. bodies were delivered to the West Yorkshire Road Car Company. They were designed and built for a minimum life of ten years. Some of them have now done over half a million miles including War service with 'perimeter seating', carrying 60 passengers. (Their designed seating capacity was 32.)

Accident damage excepted, it has not been necessary to replace a single main constructional member during the life of any of the 48 bodies, and the operator reports ''We are contemplating obtaining very considerable further useful service from them in spite of the very heavy service they were called upon to perform during the War years. All the bodies are in regular service at the present time, and will, we contemplate, so be for some years to come.''

Reproduction of a trade advertisement for long-life bodywork, one of the principal virtues of ECW bodywork and one of the instances of differing requirements due to the conflicting policies of the BET and Tilling groups.

static build system, whilst in the finishing area men worked in pairs. Manufacturing could be a very boring job, being entirely repetitive, and the monotony was relieved to a large extent by the after-hours social and sports events which management recognised as being vital to the smooth running of the factory.

Bramham is remembered as being a warm and considerate man who made a point of walking round the whole factory one morning each week, and speaking to everyone. He was a keen sportsman and encouraged the development of the company's sports facilities.

Although many tenders were submitted he was not as successful in obtaining municipal business as had been hoped and Mrs Roe was under no illusions that his defection, as she and her husband saw it, had not gone unnoticed in the staunchly loyal Yorkshire area. Apparently cricket is but one area where only Yorkshiremen can expect to make progress in Yorkshire.

In Spring 1937 a company social club and house magazine –The Hooter– made its appearance and provided an invaluable record of many events and personalities over the years. The following year Alf Cladish decided to forsake the seaside and move to the city. He is remembered as not being well when he interviewed some of those who would later make their mark on ECW, including the young Stan George and equally young Sid Wright, as far back as 1935. Whatever his problem he decided to move to Windovers, manufacturers of quality cars in Colindale, North London, and was there until his early death in 1941. His work at Colindale was connected with the production of trainer aircraft in belated recognition of the forthcoming war.

His move created an important vacancy and one wonders whether all the pieces came together by chance or whether someone in Tilling headquarters was quietly giving the

strings an occasional pull. Whatever the truth of the matter Bill Shirley was soon leaving Colin Bailey to get on with his famous and classic double-decker design at Leyland Motors' South Works, whilst Shirley headed east once more.

This time he came through the front door, as Works Manager, and his considerable experience was to be of enormous value to ECW. Writing the Foreword to the first volume in this series in 1987 he showed that he had lost none of his sharp observation and intellect, and also that his love for Leyland had not increased over the years.

He and Bramham became a formidable team and Tilling must have been well satisfied with the appointments. Work flowed into the factory and profits flowed into Tilling's coffers. There was a sense of orderliness developing, though the post-war period saw this further mature as group capacity and demand were carefully matched.

Across the country in Bristol, Arnold Romer, busy with matters pertaining to Bristol's chassis design and build, found a ready understanding from the new men. The combination of Bristol and Eastern Coach Works was to become as familiar as bread and butter, and that is just what those buses were to the factory. Solidly built, well-finished and reliable, the factory now had a regular clientele placing repeat orders for products based largely on the standard designs and in so doing creating a basis on

Bristol chassis and Eastern Coach Works bodies were to become a formidable combination in the British bus market and this stylish vehicle for Eastern Counties conveys something of the elegance of coach travel in the 'thirties. The destination arrangement in the front canopy to take the Bible layout should be noted though the folding plate itself is not in position.

which men could be sure of regular employment. In the five years up to the war 50% of the vehicles bodied in the factory were on Bristol chassis.

A change in strategy meant that advertising regained its rightful place in the scheme of things and regular full pages appeared in the trade magazines of the day. Long life was the constant theme, with illustrations of vehicles whose bodywork was sound and set for at least a ten year life. The forthcoming war would extend many bodies to almost double that life as we shall see.

Tilling's fleet engineers were involved in the design and development of the vehicles and the Bristol chassis were always described as 'engineer's buses' – the designers defied the drivers to break them. This close relationship between manufacturer and operator, dating back to Hutchinson's regime at United, virtually guaranteed satisfaction and provided security for the Bristol workforce in addition to those in Lowestoft. If the designs were conservative in some respects they were above all else reliable. Change for change's sake was not part of the philosophy, nor was introducing untested and unproven modifications to an unsuspecting operator.

In 1938 a new section leader joined the drawing office. Another Yorkshireman, he came to Lowestoft from the Humber Car Company. Prior to that he had been with Park Royal Vehicles in London and he had served his apprenticeship with Charles Roberts, bus and railway carriage builders of Wakefield. Alf Tattersall was one of the key appointments from the 'thirties and made his mark in the factory in no uncertain manner as we shall see.

There were disturbing signs that same year that political problems overseas were escalating, however, and no one in Lowestoft could close their eyes to the young Jewish and other refugees being housed in the town after being obliged to flee from their homelands. Yet as Britain faced up to the grim prospect of another war, life continued as normal in the coach factory. Large orders for North Western and Crosville were amongst many completed in 1939 and extensions to the sports field facilities also implied that things would be alright.

The sporting activities had been a very important part of the factory life for many years. The spirit of competitiveness between the various shops produced a healthy atmosphere and the 'family' tradition continued to be fostered. Other social activities included a thriving horticultural society and there were dances every Saturday evening in one or other of the canteens, with well-known bands playing. This social life was part of the integration of town and factory, for these functions were open to outsiders, and reminded everyone of the importance of the coach factory in the local economy. Bill Shirley is remembered as being a proficient and keen cricketer and tennis player, and there was universal participation in the various social activities from labourers to directors.

Extensions to the factory had allowed the output to

The interior accomodation of a mid-'thirties coach was finished to high standard and the seating was extremely comfortable. Strange that this could be achieved without the assistance of computer aided design which is considered so essential nowadays.

reach some 600 - 700 vehicles per year, and the workforce was now around 1,000. ECW was a very significant employer in the town.

Although the factory had been extended several times, and a new office block had been created, in addition to money spent on improving the sports field facilities, investment in manufacturing techniques was conspicuous by its absence. The factory depended on the traditional skills of its highly proficient craftsmen. The thorough training, up to 7 years, ensured that no one would be employed who had not learned his trade from top to bottom. The family connections have already been mentioned as has the local specialised knowledge of boatbuilding which had also been imported into the factory, very useful when mallets and chisels were still much to the fore in finishing the framing of the vehicles.

There was, it is true, a saw mill and a fitters shop with band saws and the usual array of machine tools but overall the company's success was due to the skill of the individual craftsmen and their application of traditional techniques. The design of the vehicles, whilst principally aimed at making a good product competitively so as to keep the firm profitable, determined the low level of investment in plant and equipment to make the job easier or quicker to complete.

This policy would eventually rebound when an all-engineered policy was to be introduced, but in its day it provided the maximum employment opportunities for skilled men and kept substantial profits flowing back into group coffers. The idea of ploughing in large sums of money to reduce the headcount and put people out of work played no part in the policy – if the business was profitable, and it was extremely so, why spend money?

It was this policy which created a situation where ECW was claimed at one stage to be the biggest single employer of skilled union labour in the vehicle building industry in Europe. No small claim for a seaside town hundreds of miles from nowhere as a future owner would describe it.

Through close liaison between designer, builder, operator and accountant, a well-balanced equation began to evolve which would stand the company in good stead when, in later years, supply and demand could be matched for years ahead. But, as in any well planned scheme, the politicians would upset the apple cart with nationalisation, privatisation, deregulation and ploys for vote catching. No matter that one thousand men, and their families, and the shopkeepers they bought from, all depended on the likes of ECW and Bird's Eye as major providers. The latter survived but schemes designed to achieve other objectives would eventually make ECW non-viable. That would have seemed unthinkable in 1936 and so it should have been half a century later.

Just one big happy family. Fitters at work in the 'thirties. They would be involved in making components such as pipe runs, brackets, window pans, ticket boxes, destination boxes, handrails and a host of other items. When the bonus scheme came in later years small shops could make good money from repetitive if sometimes boring work where the bigger shops would not always find it so easy.

Official photographs were usually taken outside the factory, or at Oulton Broad, in ECOC and ECW days. United had used the seafront. This view taken on 11th May 1937 shows the new company name painted above the doorways, still in the existing style, and a line of vehicles including examples for Yorkshire Traction and Westcliff. The Yorkshire Traction examples are to BET Federation design. The new frontage with the folding doors had yet to make its appearance.

One of the northern municipalities which placed an order with ECW after Bramham arrived was Burnley, Colne and Nelson Joint Transport, and this example on a Leyland torque-convertor chassis was photographed in 1939. There had been greater expectations than were achieved in the form of contracts. There are numerous hints of Roe in the shape of the bodywork, especially the upper-deck front, not altogether surprisingly perhaps.

Four

Wartime in Lowestoft and Irthlingborough

The outbreak of war in September 1939 made little immediate difference to life in the coach factory. Close on a thousand people were still employed by the Company, and buses for a wide variety of fleets were being delivered every week. During the eight months of 1939 up to the declaration of war on 3rd September some 394 vehicles were completed (based on actual deliveries during that period) and buses were collected by their customer's drivers and taken away to locations throughout the British Isles as had been the case for the previous twenty years.

Orders were still quite buoyant, though the departure of men to serve in the armed forces and the inevitable shortages of materials would affect production as the war effort became all-embracing. These shortages soon began to have an impact on construction as timber, rubber and many metals became unavailable through diversion to support the war effort. Aluminium roof panels were replaced with plywood on some vehicles, to give one example.

Yet, whilst all this drama had been unfolding, life at the factory had continued much as normal in late 1938 and in 1939. Indeed there were alterations and improvements made to the buildings – the famous brick frontage along Eastern Way with its much-photographed folding doors was constructed in the summer of 1939, and the main bodyshop had only just been extended. The bodyshop extension came in very useful during the war years, though

not for building buses, but the erection of a new grandstand to the company's sports field during January 1939 probably did little for the war effort.

The people of Lowestoft were watching the international situation very closely. During November 1938 hundreds of Jewish refugee children entered the town and were housed in the local holiday camps, these normally being closed for the winter of course, whilst arrangements were made to find them safe homes throughout Britain, America and Canada. Further reminders were never far from mind. Lowestoft was Germany's nearest British neighbour, and many had good reason to remember that on only the second day of the first war Germany had mined the waters around Southwold, some eleven miles to the south, with devastating consequences.

During August 1939 the local ARP had a trial of the town's black out precautions and events moved swiftly after that. The Sparrows Nest was commandeered by the Royal Navy even whilst the players were rehearsing, though no one was saying what was going to happen there.

Two days before the second war was declared, another contingent of children arrived, evacuated this time from London and brought by sea in paddle steamers on what seemed to them an interminable voyage. Indeed some children when asked where they had come from replied ''from England'' such had been the duration of the voyage. A further indication of what was to come was the introduction of fuel rationing at the end of September.

The town which is famous for being the first in Britain to see the morning sun now faced up to the fact that it was soon to see vistas of a less enticing nature. Lowestoft could not fail

Amongst the last vehicles to be completed at Lowestoft, seen here on 22nd May 1940 just before the enforced evacuation, was this lowbridge double-decker for Southern National. The white patch on the rear offside corner was an early indication of accident prone areas of bodywork due to the almost non-existent lighting conditions during the blackout.

to be a prime target for the marauding Messerschmitts and Dorniers which were a mere twenty minutes flying time away across the North Sea. Early in 1940 the SS Royal Crown was bombed at sea within sight of the town, the first of many naval casualties. On 21st June the first of the many air attacks on the town took place.

Nevertheless production continued in the factory for several months and customers receiving new vehicles in 1940 included North Western, East Yorkshire (with double-deckers to Beverley Bar outline to pass through that town's Gothic arch in the town walls), Bristol Tramways, and Eastern Counties with new bodies on reconditioned Leyland TD1 chassis from the early 'thirties. This latter contract was to be a foretaste of post-war activity as will be seen later.

The fall of France, and the associated decision on 26th May 1940 to evacuate all allied forces from the continent, was a devastating blow to Britain. Government response was swift and 25,000 townspeople were evacuated from Lowestoft in those early days of the war, a large percentage of the population being involved. The area was declared a restricted zone, and the beach was closed and mined, along with the fishing grounds. Miles of barbed wire suddenly appeared. Road blocks were set up and all roads into and out of the town were subject to military jurisdiction. Lowestoft seemed set to become a ghost town, entirely at the mercy of the strafing and bombing which it was powerless to resist at that time.

Anything on wheels had to be immobilised, petrol – on ration of course – was available from only one source. Empty hotels, shops, boarding houses and schools reflected the exodus, though, understandably, many people had refused to move. It was against this background that Bill Shirley received a phone call on the evening of 27th May 1940, requiring the factory to be cleared and all its contents removed from the area within 24 hours.

It is not difficult to imagine his reaction. Somewhere around 160-170 vehicles, in various stages of construction from bare chassis to fully completed buses practically ready for delivery, were in his factory. The volume and weight of stores can only be guessed, but certainly there were 1200 tons of prime timber for bodybuilding in addition to everything else. With no choice but to comply he enlisted the aid of Tilling's chairman, J F Heaton, and alternative premises at Irthlingborough (of which more later) were made available virtually immediately through the co-operation of the United Counties chief engineer, Mr Gavin.

Operators also assisted, with Eastern Counties and Eastern National providing temporary storage until the Irthlingborough premises were available a few weeks later. Brighton Hove & District, Bristol and United, amongst others, took part-completed vehicles for storage, or completion in their own workshops, using ECW employees to supervise such work, and some of these operators also provided space for those items which could not immediately be accommodated at Irthlingborough.

United undertook to provide storage space for all the machined timber which had been prepared against work in hand, and an ECW employee went to Barnard Castle to sort, label and supervise its eventual despatch to Irthlingborough.

Gordan Goodman recalls seeing the vehicles depart from Eastern Way in a macabre procession, like some grotesque pantomime, with military drivers on the temporarily lashed-up vehicles, many of which were piled high with stores and components. At the end of that day, with no further work available for them, most of the employees were discharged and there, so it seemed, the Lowestoft story would end until the war finished.

Shortly afterwards interviews were held in the town for jobs with Pressed Steel in Oxford and many ex-ECW personnel moved down to that area on war work for the duration. Many did not return, preferring to stay there when peace finally came.

A handful of employees refused to move, and no doubt a skeleton presence would be essential if only for security or firewatching. Later in 1940, after the invasion scare had receded, the military authorities allowed the factory to reopen on a very limited scale. No more than eight vehicles were allowed to be on the premises at any one time and the initial eight are believed to have been war-damaged vehicles from local fleets. There was then a spell of completing some 45 vehicles for Eastern Counties which took until the end of 1942. After that all new construction ceased completely at Lowestoft until the end of 1945 for the 1946 post-war deliveries, though repair work and manufacture of small items for Irthlingborough continued. Women were employed on various jobs now, including painting and other areas where they would never have been seen previously.

On 6th January 1941 schools were authorised to reopen for those children who had not been evacuated – or had returned – and later that year, in August, the first British Restaurant in the town was opened. Interviews with retired employees reveal that by September 1941, if not before, apprentices were being taken on at ECW, confirming that production had been continuing, albeit in a small way. They included Gerald Vincent who over the next 40 years worked as an electrician, finally retiring in 1987, Brian Ratcliffe a sheet metal worker from January 1941 to November 1986 and Gordon Goodman who in his 37 years worked in the experimental shop for 25 years, was a shop steward for 18 years and served on the branch committee of the NUVB for 20 years. Their various recollections of the early days and first hand experience of the changes over the years have helped enormously in setting down this story.

There seems to be an assumption that following the instruction to evacuate the coach works and a substantial portion of the populace, and with the enforced cessation of fishing, Lowestoft effectively closed down for the war. In bus building terms this might be nearly true but in other respects it could not be further from the truth!

Events in the town itself had been much more dramatic. What changed the whole situation so very significantly was almost certainly the boldness of one man, Commodore Bill Piercey, officer commanding HMS Europa, the 'stone frigate' which acted as central depot for the men of the Royal Naval Patrol Service and whose personnel were to train, equip and man the trawlers used for the crucial mine-sweeping and anti-submarine patrol work for the rest of the war. This was what Sparrows Nest was required for.

There were, on average, some 7,000 of these men in the town at any time, and the seaside landladies and housewives returned to provide accommodation for them. It is recorded that this naval presence alone was responsible for making this the most prosperous, if not the happiest, time in the town's history.

Many of the evacuees, which included some 600 children, had been moved to Glossop in Derbyshire and many were to marry and stay in that area. One Northerner who made the trip the other way, naval rating Philip Morton, was billeted next door to, and later married, Audrey Ashton-Stray, the former Town Clerk's daughter. Such was the level of activity in dealing with the provision of accommodation for this huge shifting population that a full-time staff of 25 people were employed in the billeting office to keep pace.

Sadly the Germans were not unaware of this massive naval effort and its tremendous importance to the war effort. Lord Haw Haw, the German propagandist, frequently referred to the 'Sparrows in the Nest', that being the headquarters of the unit, and the frequent and savage bombing of the town reflects its military importance. Strangely, although many houses, shops and public buildings were bombed out of existence, Sparrows Nest itself escaped virtually unscathed despite the lighthouse on the road which they could hardly fail to miss seeing as they came in on their bombing runs.

Shipbuilding had also reassumed a great importance, the Patrol Service needing wooden (non-magnetic) boats for mine sweeping and convoy escort duties, and men paid-off from the Coach Factory and who moved to the boatyards in the town and at Oulton Broad would also have been forced to take cover on many occasions to avoid the raiders.

The lighthouse and entrance to Sparrows Nest, a well-known local landmark.

Commodore Piercey's stand against the Admiralty – who wanted to move the patrol base to safer shores in Shrewsbury – may have had something to do with his superior knowledge of the difficulty involved in navigating ocean going trawlers into that town. We shall never know, but his belief in the need to show courage and determination against the foe by remaining in Lowestoft was supported by the long-suffering people of the town who were bombed without warning on numerous occasions in the early wartime months. Later, heavy guns deterred the planes and gave greater opportunity for escape into the air raid shelters. There were more than 2,000 'alerts' in the 2,075 days that the war lasted.

The small band of staff working at Eastern Way occupied only a small portion of the factory. As mentioned they produced components for Irthlingborough, using some of the machinery which had not been taken away when the factory was virtually cleared. Replacement mudguards were a steady line apparently, thanks to the blackout restrictions. Another, more unusual contract, covered the repair and refurbishment of the metal folding 'bible' indicator plates favoured by some Tilling fleets and seen on page 24. Brian Ratcliffe recalls 'a small mountain' of these being delivered, and spending many hours soldering up damaged components.

Sid Paignton, the plant electrician, was charged with the task of removing fuses and key items from all machinery at the end of each day and secreting these in the air raid shelters or elsewhere where they would not be found if the expected invasion had taken place.

Air raid and firewatching became an important part of the daily – and nightly – routine and many rounds of unexploded cannon shells were found on the factory roof and in the yards. The fact that only one serious incident occurred, when incendiaries set part of the body shops alight, raises the question as to whether the enemy were aware of the factory's low strategic importance. Domestic dwelling and shops were apparently given a much greater priority by the Luftwaffe.

Gradually the small workforce increased its production of components, and also handled the occasional body repair. Elsewhere in the factory army personnel were servicing their vehicles, whilst the Royal Air Force had a mess for the barrage balloon detachment based on the company sports field. Camouflage netting was being manufactured in the erecting shops and heartbreaking piles of furniture from bombed-out homes in the town were being stored in the bodyshops.

A regular routine throughout the war was the delivery of manufactured components from Lowestoft to Irthlingborough. Each Saturday afternoon the work's Armstrong Siddley pickup made its journey through the road blocks and out of the blockaded town to the other factory, and each Sunday afternoon it returned with Dick Tyrell at the wheel. Later in the war Fred Freeman did the driving. This production routine was a natural extension of the famous 'batch system', particularly as space was at a premium at the shadow factory.

It seemed a shame to waste the space in the otherwise

empty vehicle on its return journey and, as Irthlingborough was at the centre of the shoe manufacturing industry, some neat organisation ensured that Lowestoft people in the know were never short of new shoes, usually (but not always!) 'seconds', they would hasten to add.

The increase in work levels at Lowestoft brought Albert McCall back from Irthlingborough to take over the position of Works Manager and to join Freddie Thompson who was looking after administration and Ted Godley who was in charge of the saw mill and also the factory fire service. Others who are remembered from this period include Harold Pilling for his multi-faceted role – from sounding the Air Raid warning Klaxon on the roof to

Freddie Thompson was featured in *The Hooter* in 1950 and his career made fascinating reading. After being involved with aircraft in the First War he joined Mann Egerton in Norwich becoming principal assistant to the chief designer before moving to United as a salesman in 1926. He was transferred to the drawing office at Lowestoft and remained there for over 25 years. During the war he was in charge of the Lowestoft factory.

running the canteen, paying out the wages and, meantimes, organising those little jobs which would otherwise have ceased 'for the duration'. New or good quality timber was non-existent, of course, like many other commodities. Yet, strangely, Harold's local church was apparently able to acquire a new lectern and some splendid chairs tastefully upholstered in best Tilling green leather. . .

There was a bonus scheme even during the war and the local shopkeepers became aware of the increased spending power of the workforce after the quarterly pay out, though whether there was much to buy in wartime days was another matter.

An important event which occurred in 1942 may not have registered with many of the workforce at either of the factories but during that year TBAT split and ECW became 100% Tilling controlled. Some of the bus companies changed from control by Tilling to control by BET and North Western was one such company which would soon be debarred from taking ECW bodywork following the later ramifications of this move.

Another significant move at this time was the setting up of Bristol Commercial Vehicles Ltd as a separate entity,

with Sir Frederick Heaton, Major Chapple and Arnold J Romer as Directors.

As the war progressed and the tide slowly turned in the allies favour, matters eased somewhat. The restriction on the numbers of vehicles that could be held on the premises was raised from the aforementioned eight to thirty in 1943. In July of that same year, in another move reflecting the easing of tension, the south beach was reopened to the public, a facility probably appreciated a year later when more children were evacuated into the town from London as the V1 'Doodlebug' rockets began to cause havoc in the Capital. In the following month, on 23rd August 1944, the ban on entry to coastal areas was lifted and around the same time all restrictions on numbers of vehicles on the factory premises were lifted. The way back to something approaching normality could be envisaged, and free movement would enable people from outside the town to come back to work in the factory.

During 1944 George Crisp, known to many if not all the people in the factory in his later days as the Quality Control Inspector, joined ECW working at Irthlingborough. George's grandfather and father both worked at ECW, as did his son. Another man with family connections throughout the factory was Denis Mitchell who started at Irthlingborough the previous year and both have many memories of the changes seen over the years. Both men were interviewed in 1994 and were very critical of the later years at Lowestoft when control had passed out of local management's hands. George was particularly bitter that the closure of the factory had, as in so many other cases throughout the country, deprived local youngsters of the prospect of a skilled job in the town.

On 30th June 1944 production of the Bristol K chassis was resumed though it was to be some months before Lowestoft received any for bodying. Denis Mitchell was one who returned from Irthlingborough in March 1945 as the build up of personnel in the main factory got under way. Many of the men were still away in the forces, many others would leave to carry out military service, and so there was a steady stream of young and older men coming and going to and from both factories. Today the personnel and wages departments would need a computer with a database to cope with all these machinations but doubtless the office staff of the day took it all in their stride with fountain pens, and typewriters with carbon copy paper, long before the age of the photocopier or the computer.

Another very welcome sign was the resumption of fishing as Lowestoft resumed its peacetime role as a fishing port once all the mines from the fishing grounds or access lanes had been removed or blown up.

By the end of the war in 1945 there were some 200 people working at ECW Lowestoft and quite quickly the numbers were increased as the foremen and other people were brought back from Irthlingborough and others gradually returned from the forces. The return was organised to some extent on the availability of accommodation since not everyone still had a home in Lowestoft. The management team returned early in 1946 and production of the L and K-type bodies then began.

IRTHLINGBOROUGH

Meanwhile, whilst all this activity had been taking place in Lowestoft, a very different situation had developed at Irthlingborough. After the macabre procession had left Lowestoft on 28th May 1940, the vehicles and components were stored before delivery at the end of June to the one-time United Counties bus depot which Tilling's Chairman had been able to secure.

Tucked away almost out of sight behind a row of terraced cottages, and surrounded by trees, its narrow access from the Finedon Road was through a gap between the houses. It was too small to accommodate all the vehicles, and, as mentioned, some were diverted to customers for storage or completion, but it had an erecting shop and the necessary pits to allow limited production to continue.

Only a few days later, in early June 1940, approximately 150 workers were taken on. Some 120 of these were key ex-Lowestoft personnel who were transported to work by road each day until they were able to find local accommodation in 'digs', and local people over military age were also employed. The ECW management consisted of Bill Bramham, General Manager; Bill Shirley, Works Manager; Ralph Sugden, Commercial Manager; Frank Bayliss, Stores Officer; John Ross, Technical Officer; Ronnie Statham, Development Engineer, and Ronald Jones in the drawing office with Alf Tattersall.

Several years later the company house magazine *The Hooter* carried some interesting reminiscences concerning Irthlingborough. Apparently June 1940 was hot and dry – exceptionally so – and a grass fire got out of hand and nearly burned the place down before any work began.

Later that year the severe winter made its mark and Lowestoft people in digs in the Irthlingborough area reckoned they had never been so cold. The damp chill was infinitely worse than the biting east coast winds, but the winters of 1940 and 1941 were bad everywhere of course with blizzards and considerable falls of snow throughout the country.

Notwithstanding these privations lasting friendships developed and continued after everyone returned home. Regular visits between the two factories also became a feature of the sports club's activities for several years after the war.

Meanwhile, in the factory, the work of completing those vehicles which could be completed after delivery from their temporary storage was then followed by another problem as non-military chassis production ceased at Bristol (and everywhere else), under Ministry orders, thus allowing all efforts to be concentrated on wartime needs.

There was, however, a steady and ever-increasing amount of repair work. Bristol was one of several cities severely blitzed during the early part of 1941 and many of its buses were sent to be repaired at Irthlingborough. Other fleets suffered similarly, but there was also a need to refurbish life-expired vehicles to allow them to provide further service. This influx of repair work was, apparently, to prove significant in shaping the Company's post-war policy. The work force was increased and recruitment of apprentices continued. Gus Halkes, who had been at Lowestoft since Eastern Counties days, was one of the men who spent the war years at Irthlingborough and he recalls the poor condition of the vehicles coming in for repair and the ingenuity needed to rebuild them.

Most of the buses coming to Irthlingborough would be from Tilling fleets, and therefore timber framed, but there were apparently some metal-framed examples, perhaps from Bristol or Lincolnshire, the latter now a Tilling fleet. The shortcomings of metal-framing were clearly demonstrated as these vehicles came into the factory. Once the panels were taken off there were large expanses of fresh air where steel framing should have been evident. People working there recall that some of these were Leyland bodies but wartime records are not too clear. Certainly there were Leyland bodies of an earlier vintage, 'piano-fronted' Titans from around 1930, but they were timber framed or composite bodies.

These vehicles came in for repair or rehabilitation work, in some instances being converted from open-staircase layout, having sliding windows fitted to replace the wind-down variety and often losing their piano fronts at the same time. Coaches, not needed during the war, were converted to service buses, and perimeter seating was installed in many hundreds of vehicles to allow more passengers to be carried by increasing the area available for standees. John Ross, the technical officer, had conceived this idea which allowed upwards of 60 people to travel in a 35 seater bus.

It was largely thanks to such innovative work that Irthlingborough was able to remain as a bus factory and did not pass into the hands of the Ministry of Aircraft Production or other Government departments. Park Royal and Duple had by this time both come under MAP control for the construction and assembly of aircraft or their components. In November 1941 the Irthlingborough premises were purchased from United Counties for the sum of £17,500, having merely been occupied by ECW up to that time.

Some vehicles which came in for work classified as repair were in fact quite extensively rebuilt and despite wartime shortages of rubber, windows glazed in that material made their first appearance, giving a pointer to post-war intentions.

Whatever the origin of the particular bodies Bill Shirley had seen the beginnings of this corrosion problem in Leyland nearly a decade earlier. Indeed it was the very reason Spurrier had head-hunted Colin Bailey from Met-Cam, to stop the rot in the Leyland metal-framed bodies. Clearly, metal framing and jig manufactured components had much to offer, but only if adequate protection against corrosion could be ensured. It seems likely that there was plenty of time to consider the situation since repair work would hardly over-tax the management's combined talents one supposes. Clearly, with a very able design team all under one small roof, ideas would flow and here we appear to have the makings of the Tilling 'Think Tank', to use a phrase popular in later years.

There was a consensus that aluminium framing must be seriously investigated, since it would not corrode and should be capable of improving on the already well-respected 'long-life' bodies for which ECW had become renowned. It had the additional bonus of being lighter than wood or steel. As the Ministry of Supply wartime utility body designs came into the factory for those few completely new bodies which Irthlingborough would build, much thought was clearly given as to the design, construction and material content of the bodies ECW would produce once the war was over. A design of longitudinal waistrail which allowed the pillars to be threaded though it was developed and patented. It was the fundamental feature of the post-war bodies and provided great strength, running as it did the full length of the vehicles.

A project of a completely different nature was the building of two experimental gas powered single-deckers. There was a shortage of petrol largely due to the activities of the German U-boats which were sinking the tankers bringing in vital supplies from overseas. A government instruction to bus companies to convert 10% of their fleets to run on gas produced by burning anthracite in a small trailer towed behind the vehicle was received with no enthusiasm in most fleets, for the loss of power, particularly with a diesel engine, was considerable. In the Tilling Group, however, Chairman J F Heaton took the matter very seriously and made it his business to see that the instruction was obeyed. His persistence earned him his knighthood after the war had ended.

The experimental single-deckers were an attempt to produce a self-contained unit without the cumbersome trailer, and two Bristol L chassis with Gardner 6LW engines were earmarked for the project. The bodywork was largely to Ministry of Supply utility design, with front entrance and a rear compartment with external doors giving access to the gas producing plant. The first one be completed was delivered to Eastern National and its fellow went to Eastern Counties. Although the vehicles were apparently reasonably successful this line of action was not pursued and they remained unique. As fuel supplies eased the producer gas project was abandoned by the government – to the enormous relief of most operators –

and the two experimental vehicles were rebuilt during 1946 to conventional diesel configuration.

Despite the pressures of war it was necessary for the Tilling Group to plan for what would obviously be a huge demand for new buses once the war ended. Bill Bramham, like many people, had been pessimistic about the likely outcome of the war, an attitude shown in his initial lack of enthusiasm for Albert McCall's suggestion that all the dismantled Lowestoft machinery at Irthlingborough should be overhauled and refurbished, and then greased and stored until it could be reinstated. Bramham eventually agreed and this far-seeing action by McCall was one of the main factors in assisting a speedy return to post-war production in Lowestoft.

Notwithstanding any apprehension about the war's outcome, the team pressed on. It was recognised that to meet the pent-up demand the factory would be stretched to its limits and would have to maximise its resources. In many ways it was a golden opportunity to plan for more streamlined production, with few if any variations from standard, in the immediate post-war period.

Other manufacturers were thinking along similar lines, of course, and Leyland dropped its single-deck range completely until 1950, allowing all production to be concentrated on one double-deck design which would be available in lowbridge or full-height form.

Here ECW would have an enormous advantage over the rest of the bus manufacturing industry. It had, effectively, a captive market, but one whose customers still had some say, through their fleet engineers, as to the design and construction of the products. No one was under any illusion that the end of the war would mean things would be easy, but the scope for reorganising the Lowestoft factory to deal with such standardisation, and an accurately predictable order book, must have been a welcome prospect in the gloomy wartime days.

By coincidence at least two other people germane to ECW's future were also becoming involved in jig-assembled aluminium framed body construction, though for a very different mode of transport. Stan George, now an airframe fitter in the RAF, was learning a great deal about aluminium construction, including stresses and frame maintenance. He went on a course to RAF Halton, only to find his instructor was none other than Sid Wright, his recent fellow apprentice, now an instructor in airframe maintenance and repair work, and the production of Instruction Manuals, and recently posted to Halton after a spell on airframe

The rear view of one of the gas-producer buses shows the metal doors which gave access to the anthracite burner within. Body design generally followed MoS Utility specification but some features of post-war construction were developed from this.

construction in Blackpool. Sid was also to spend much time with safety equipment, useful training for his later career.

It would be some years before Stan George would become Chief Designer and Sid Wright Works Manager but, without doubt, those were significant days for both men and for ECW's post-war production.

In another twist to the story, problems at Short Brothers in Rochester during 1942/3 gave cause for grave concern at the Ministry of Aircraft Production, and Sir Stafford Cripps quickly arranged for Bill Bramham from ECW and Arnold Romer from Bristol to be seconded to the board of directors and to sort out the problems. Romer, it will be remembered, had been in charge of the Coach Factory whilst it was under ECOC control, but had left to go to the Bristol Constructional Works at Brislington in 1936.

Before the war Shorts had been bus and trolleybus builders, but it was their flying boat expertise and aircraft production that was now at stake. They had also experimented with aluminium framing for bus bodies. Bramham and Romer were not to return to their normal occupations until 1945 but both men must have learned much about the properties and manufacture of aluminium sections for body framing whilst at Rochester. With Bramham's enforced removal from ECW Bill Shirley was promoted to Deputy General Manager (Production) and Ralph Sugden to Deputy General Manager (Commercial).

The Patents taken out in Bramham's name in 1942 before his secondment in 1943 clearly show that he, and therefore ECW, had taken the matter of metal framing some way forward before the move to Shorts. Still there remained the problem of corrosion but the new techniques in manufacturing aluminium extrusions being developed for aircraft production were to provide the key. ECW's management decided they would base the post-war bodies on aluminium framing once they had proved the designs, and once the necessary materials could be obtained in quantity.

During this time at Irthlingborough, Alf Tattersall began to make his mark, working with John Ross, Ronnie Statham and Ronald Jones in the drawing office. New body construction was only allowed to proceed at Irthlingborough because of the continuing risk to Lowestoft and the beginnings of the post-war double-decker body began to emerge as vehicles were fitted with replacement bodywork. Wilts and Dorset, Hants and Dorset and Brighton, Hove and District were three operators to take bodywork which would later be recognised as being precursors of the K-type body on chassis dating back to the early 'thirties.

The origin of the post-war K body is clear to trace, coming as it did from the ECW interpretation of the wartime utility design. This emanated from the organisation set up by the Ministry of Supply and Ministry of War Transport in co-operation with manufacturers and operators to draw up the specification for wartime buses. The actual responsibility passed to the National Federation of Vehicle Trades and Operators Joint Technical and Advisory Committee, set up in 1941, whose President was Mr W R Black, Director and General Manager of Park Royal. The origin of the single-deck body was a different story and that vehicle must surely rank as one of the outstanding and classic single-decker bus designs of all time. If anyone knows of a better claim to such a title, or to the L's designer, the authors would be pleased to hear from them.

With commendable speed the Irthlingborough-designed single-deck L body was put into production as soon as chassis became available from Bristol in 1945. Albert McCall was placed in charge of the Irthlingborough factory as the rest of the management returned to Lowestoft, and, under his supervision, three of these bodies were produced each week, on average, for the next three years from Irthlingborough. The temporary, emergency, facility had finally come into its own, and a substantial order for United was amongst those which kept the Northamptonshire workforce busy in the immediate post-war period.

In the next chapter we shall see how the two factories coped with the Tilling Group's requirements, and other non-Tilling orders, following the return to peacetime conditions.

Brighton, Hove and District had had new vehicles on order in the early days of the war but the chassis were cancelled and the bodies, when eventually built in 1943, were placed on AEC Regent chassis of 1931 vintage. Note the wartime requirements of masked headlamps and white-painted mudguards.

Five

Post-War Production 1946-1965

The end of the war was greeted with relief, and then an awareness of the need to press on with rebuilding the war torn economy. Transport featured high on the task list but exports were an even greater priority to obtain money through overseas sales with which to pay the huge cost of beating the Axis powers.

The Irthlingborough factory moved swiftly into peacetime mode and the factory became a one-model production line with three single-decker Bristol L's being produced each week. Nearly three hundred went to United's fleet over the next two years – 'like a line that never ends' as a certain Professor Higgins would later say. As the Lowestoft factory got back to normal and employees returned from the forces so the Irthlingborough factory was wound down to be closed in 1952, the same year L chassis production ceased.

The method of determining who returned to Lowestoft first was partly determined by the availability of accommodation. Not everyone had somewhere to live in Lowestoft, some houses having been bombed for instance. Gradually the situation was sorted and all who wished to return did so.

Over 45 years after bus production and assembly had been moved from there the buildings still house band saws, guillotines and folding presses, and large quantities of timber and aluminium still pass through, for in 1995 the present owners manufacture static homes – large non-mobile caravan types of construction – and the site looks very much as it did during the war. Only a smart new brick-built office and reception area, in front the original buildings, give the game away, The other corrugated clad buildings in their drab black paint would be instantly recognised by anyone who had worked there in the 'forties.

Back in Lowestoft in 1945 the need was to maximise output as soon as possible. The new models were in full swing, 'any colour you like as long as it's red or green' seemed to be the yardstick. What was lacking, however, was a supply of good timber. Burma teak and the like were unobtainable. Oak and elm were available but not seasoned, and there was no time to wait. The early post-war bodies were the worst the factory had ever made. Externally they looked fine with their smooth lines, simple yet neat liveries, and destination boxes carrying blinds which left no room for doubt as to the vehicle's intentions. Underneath the skin it was another matter and before long the unseasoned timber began to cause problems.

In many people's opinion the design of the Tilling group's standard post-war single-decker was an outright winner. Neat, well proportioned, even with its large Tilling destination boxes, it became one of the all-time classics, very much as the smaller Bedford Duple OB was doing. This example was photographed by ECW's photographer at Oulton Broad, before it left for a spell at Irthlingborough to be examined by staff there before production began. Later it would make its trip to Grange Road, Darlington, but post-war shortages meant that there were no United blinds available when it was photographed and so Eastern Counties blinds were fitted instead. Crosville single and double-decker vehicles were similarly treated at this time – ah the benefits of standardisation. The lower blinds, one-piece initially, were extraordinarily long and the poor quality post-war timber was simply not up to the stresses imposed by the winding mechanism on the vehicles. Some operators solved the problem very quickly by painting over the glass but Tilling Group were not impressed. A later scheme divided the lower blind as will be seen.

The coach factory was not alone in this problem though at Leeds they admitted to having hidden some timber out of sight of ministry eyes in 1940, ready for peacetime production. Leyland and others building in steel pressed on regardless, but Leyland's steel-framed bodies rotted too and it was a bad time for all bodybuilders.

On the good side there was a huge demand for buses and ECW was able to apply very rigid control over what it would allow its customers to purchase. Tilling fleets were already committed to the standard Lowestoft products but even 'outside' customers taking vehicles ordered before or during the war, or those ordered after the war, found themselves having very little say in style or design.

The situation was assisted by the standardisation on the Bristol K and L chassis though Guy, Leyland and AEC models came through from outstanding orders or for non-Tilling fleets. The single-deck body in its express form was the closest option to a coach available at that time. At the end of the 'forties almost 70% of the output was of double-deckers and the workforce had risen to some 1,300 – 300 more than the peak before the war. The improved production methods and standard designs had allowed output to increase far more than the corresponding proportional increase in labour. To cater for the increased workforce a new canteen was opened in 1949.

The increase in production was being achieved in the face of shortages of raw materials – exports still had priority – and power cuts as demand exceeded supply. The unease in the world political situation resulted in a massive rearmament programme with a consequent return to shortages of raw materials. Labour was also in short supply; a statistic quoted in *The Hooter* recorded some 400,000 unfilled job vacancies being available nationally. The same article made a strong plea for people who wished to do so to be allowed to work until they were finally ready to retire, thus retaining skills and experience and helping to avoid creating vacancies! A far cry from today's situation and one which the younger generation may find difficult to comprehend.

The post-war range: standardisation on a scale never imagined before the war. Highbridge and lowbridge double-deckers, express and stage carriage single-deckers. Red or Green. Even the upholstery was common to both liveries.

Below centre: Bill Shirley was also Chairman of the Sports and Social Club and in that capacity he performed the official opening ceremony of the new canteen at the end of 1949.

Foot: Typical of the rebodied double-deckers supplied to many customers was this pre-war Leyland, now fitted with the post-war K-type body and supplied to Ribble Motor Services at Preston before Nationalisation prevented non-Tilling group operators from buying ECW bodies.

The Economy Factory

Another means of increasing throughput was the opening of the 'Economy Factory' at the south end of the town in some rather dilapadated buildings in amongst other factories. Trim and finishing operations were transferred there as also was the staff dining room. The factory was under the control of Jack Baldwin, run from his 'wheelhouse', and in addition to the manufacture and upholstery of seats and trim, the wooden seat frames were also constructed here.

The small complex also included pattern making facilities under the eagle eye of Bill Moore, wood and paint stores, first-aid and canteen, and the necessary machinery for production. A row of lock-up garages provided storage space for extruded aluminium sections. Unfortunately, it has not been possible to ascertain the precise date when this facility closed and everyone moved back to Eastern Way, and, strangely, even some ECW people seem to be completely unaware of the existence of this factory.

As a consequence of the increased workforce and extended main factory, additional clocking on points were provided with a new facility, pulsed slave clocks driven from a master unit to ensure absolute consistency throughout. This may have been linked to the abortive, much derided, work-study scheme which attempted to introduce measured day rate in place of the bonus. Sid Wright, as Labour Officer, recalls no one wanted it – neither men, union or management. Everyone recalls it as a colossal waste of money, entirely without precedent in the company's history.

The Economy Factory as seen in the *The Hooter* magazine's notes each month.

Some single-deck business came to the factory through Leyland's decision, mentioned earlier, to concentrate entirely on double-deckers, and orders for Western Welsh were amongst those which were completed on Leyland Tiger chassis. Municipal business included some double-deckers for Lowestoft Corporation, on AEC chassis, and also some single and double-deckers on Bristol chassis for Aberdare. BET orders were responsible for double and single-deckers, with examples going to East Kent, Ribble and North Western, amongst others. It was a time of great variety and tremendous throughput.

Despite all this activity ECW's management must have been very frustrated. They recognised the problems with poor timber and foresaw what the outcome would be. They also knew what they wanted to do, indeed an experimental body section of one double-deck bay had been produced in aluminium and was set up in the factory. It was passed regularly by the returning drawing office staff, including Stan George, as they went about their daily tasks.

The opportunity to put theory into practice came with an overseas order for Bristol L's where a timber framed body would not be acceptable due to the action of termites which ate their way through the timber framing. The order was placed by a Johannesburg dealer and because of the export drive the necessary authority to proceed was obtained

The export order for 50 single-deck buses for South Africa was significant in that it opened the door to aluminium body framing at a time when restrictions on availability of materials for the home market would probably otherwise have kept it closed. The order was also seen as opening the door to a promising export market but that door was slammed shut by a Conservative requirement that the Transport Act which brought in nationalisation should preclude the manufacture of and supply to non-BTC customers by BTC manufacturers. This was another instance of party political meddling by people who in trying to protect one group mortally wound another.

and the sections and extrusions were ordered. From this order the change to aluminium framing was to be implemented as soon as practicable and the unseasoned timber bodies would become just a bad dream. Until they came back for replacement with new bodies a few years later, that is. Some while after the South African vehicles entered service a letter was received at the coach factory stating that these vehicles were considered to be the finest that had been imported into that country to that date. Praise indeed!

As men were demobbed they were able to return to their former employment and one who would play a significant part in the post-war years was Sid Wright, who had returned to the factory in 1946 following his spell in the RAF. Sid recalled that he was in a difficult position, like many others. He had gone to war as a lad, his apprenticeship not yet complete, then returned on a 'resumed apprenticeship' at 1/11d per hour after six years during which he had attained the rank of sergeant and had been in charge of training men. Clearly he was now too mature to be a junior in the drawing office and he gradually found himself being groomed by Ralph Sugden for higher things. He had been in charge of Instruction Manual production relating to aluminium airframe maintenance whilst in the forces and had spent some time at RAF Halton as an Instructor. Sugden brought him into contact with Alf Tattersall, chief designer at that time, who subsequently moved him into the drawing office.

Others felt the need to spread their wings to advance their careers. Albert McCall had been in charge at Irthlingborough but left to take up a position with Northern Coachbuilders in Newcastle in 1947. In contrast in November of that year Bill Shirley was promoted to Deputy General Manager of Eastern Coach Works just before the next major shake-up when the Tilling Group found itself nationalised from New Year's Day 1948.

Nationalisation

One of the many people who had no stomach for this turn of events was Bill Bramham. Working for a state-owned concern was not in his scheme of things and on 13th May his forthcoming departure – to NCB at Newcastle – was announced.

A principal cause for concern in the changed situation was the restriction on taking orders from non-nationalised customers. Bramham must have been able to see that the good times could not continue at the rate of the late 'forties and once operators had caught up with overdue fleet replacements the overall level of business would start to drop. The last thing any management wanted was a restriction on who they could or could not supply. The BET business would be lost, as would that from municipalities and independents, though these latter two were perhaps not so crucial. A more detailed explanation of the complex situation will be found in *ECW – 1946-1965* also published by Venture Publications Ltd, but suffice to say that this was the start of a chain of events where the coach factory found itself powerless to shape fully its own future.

Bramham duly left and Bill Shirley was immediately appointed to the position of GM whilst Joseph Rodhouse took Shirley's earlier position as Works Manager. After all this upheaval things settled down for a little while until Rodhouse left in 1950 and Alf Tattersall took the reins in the factory – and held them very tightly for the next 20 years. Tattersall is remembered with mixed feelings – a difficult man, not easily given to listening, never one to give a quick decision where money was concerned, and yet brilliant at his job and completely dedicated to keeping people in work.

Rodhouse, as the new Works Manager, saw that there was a need for someone to be responsible for internal sales, to monitor costs and ensure customers were charged for additional work carried out or modifications made, previously Sugden's domain, and Sid Wright was moved to this position as estimator, working with Frank Bayliss the chief buyer.

Tilling policy was to buy large quantities of raw materials such as timber, aluminium and copper when prices were low, and then to stockpile against rising prices. There was ample space for storage but the policy required tight control of the stores.

ECW policy was to stay with a small number of suppliers, ensuring that price, quality and delivery were always maintained though multiple sourcing of some items did take place, notably paint. When the National Bus Company was formed in later years it took over the responsibility for specifications and the placing of contracts.

Between 1947 and 1950 the percentage of aluminium used in the body construction gradually increased, though the external body design remained largely unchanged. This meant a change in manufacturing techniques and many men previously employed on machining timber were retrained to work with aluminium though there was, of course, still considerable timber in the bodywork – not least the floors.

A welcome return to internal communications both at Lowestoft and with Irthlingborough and the Economy Factory was the reappearance of the monthly magazine *The Hooter* from March 1950.

Amendments to the regulations concerning the length and width of buses were introduced at various times between 1948 and the late 'fifties and vehicles became longer and wider. Nevertheless the standard single- and double-deck designs, suitably updated to take advantage of the revised dimensions, remained in production until 1955 and 1957 respectively though mainstream production of the L chassis had actually finished in 1952.

In October 1949 ECW and Bristol Commercial Vehicles made a tremendous leap forward when they introduced their prototype Lodekka – literally a low decker. They had finally devised a design to eliminate once-and-for-all the tiresome side gangway layout necessary for buses operating in areas with low railway bridges, though the initial concept of a twin drive-line either side of a lowered central gangway was later revised.

Once the prototypes had proved the soundness of the concept, orders flowed in from the Tilling fleets and in 1953, after a batch of pre-production models had been placed in service, the model was put into full production. The programme had been thoroughly investigated and fully proven before operators were supplied with bulk orders and this operator-supplier relationship to which reference has already been made was once again showing benefits for operator and manufacturer. No costly campaign changes here!

The men behind the Lodekka were John Ross and Oliver Pease and their enormous talent put Tilling head-and-shoulders above the other chassis manufacturers. Stan George was also busy in the drawing offfice at this time, working on a new concept, for Eastern Counties had a need for some lightweight vehicles and the earlier Beadle chassisless design was judged unsuitable. Stan had worked on airframe construction during the war, subsequently moving on demob to Gloucester Aircraft at Hucklecote where he worked on the forerunner of the Javelin. In 1947 he was requested to return to ECW by the Ministry of Labour, who were placing people into their old jobs where possible, and his experience of aluminium structures and stress calculation was to be invaluable in the coach factory. The ECOC vehicles were successful but the project was overtaken by the more significant LS lightweight semi-integral model which ECW and Bristol were developing for a wider market within Tilling fleets.

Meanwhile the K and L models were still in build but in May 1950 the first ECW post-war coach made its appearance. The projecting radiator of the Bristol chassis gave it a rugged appearance but an enclosed radiator design was introduced shortly afterwards when the model was extended to 30ft x 8ft, producing what some operators described as their best ever coaches. Significantly, they reverted to being timber framed, probably because the anticipated orders were insufficient to justify expenditure on new extrusions. The curved waistrail may also have been a consideration, easier to produce in timber than aluminium.

The project apparently stemmed from Bill Shirley's determination not to let business go to competitors and, interestingly, it was recorded at the time that 'ECW was a bus builder, not a coach builder'. Some of the old hands must have shaken their heads at that statement.

An initial order for six for Crosville resulted in other customers' orders being

The Lodekka's *raison d'etre* was the desire to eliminate the awkward side-gangway layout on lowbridge buses. In a clever move ECW's John Ross and Oliver Pease, working with the Bristol engineers, achieved this by revising the transmission layout and dropping the lower-deck gangway, killing two birds with one stone by also making access much easier as can be seen. The lower view of one of the prototypes shows the affinity to the K-type body, but with centre gangways to each deck in a low height configuration.

The first post-war coach design, in 1950, was a handsome vehicle, even more so when the opportunity was taken to tidy up the frontal design at the same time as the regulations allowed the vehicle to built to 8ft wide by 30ft long.

placed and 205 of the 'banana boats' or, more properly, 'Queen Marys' were built during 1951/2. Once again ECW had shown that left to themselves they could build anything, and make money out of it.

A factory outing to the Commercial Motor Show in London on 23rd September gave Irthlingborough staff an opportunity to sample one of these new coaches at first hand when United Counties thoughtfully allocated one for the trip. They were recorded as being extremely impressed. There was also a works outing from Lowestoft on the same day and an opportunity arose for a reunion of people who had previously worked together.

In December 1950 the first LS vehicle was produced, having its engine mounted below the floor, and thus increasing the space available for passengers – it was now possible to seat 44 passengers in a single-decker bus. The switch to semi-integral vehicles increased the work content at Lowestoft and also demanded new skills but, as always, the workforce found no problems in adapting to change.

Once again no major investment was required and production continued to be achieved through high levels of in-house skill and expertise. As customers took quantities of the new LS model so production of the L was scaled down. Some conversions were later carried out whereby the L was rebuilt with full-fronted bodywork and there had also been front and dual-door configurations of the bodywork but the new underfloor models were to render front engined chassis obsolete almost overnight.

Some variety was introduced to the factory in 1951 with a batch of sight-seeing coaches on AEC chassis, delivered to London Transport and to Tillings for work in connection with the Festival of Britain which was held on London's South Bank that year. Another order for London, handled in 1953, was for 84 small Guy single-deckers but after that apart from a solitary Routemaster double-deck coach, and later some LHs, London orders dried up uuntil almost the end of production at Lowestoft. During 1952 a batch of 50 cabs for Bristol lorries was produced, being mounted on the chassis in Bristol.Some platform bodies for the same type of chassis were built at Irthlingborough that same year. Unfortunately no further orders followed.

Apprentices were encouraged at ECW, as in most large companies, by the presentation of awards for good work. Trades open to them at this time included Woodcutting machinists; Bodymakers and Finishers; Sheet Metal Workers and Panel beaters; Coach Fitters; Coach Painters; Trimmers; Electricians. Note that transport would be provided home after the evening event 'at moderate fares', no largesse here!

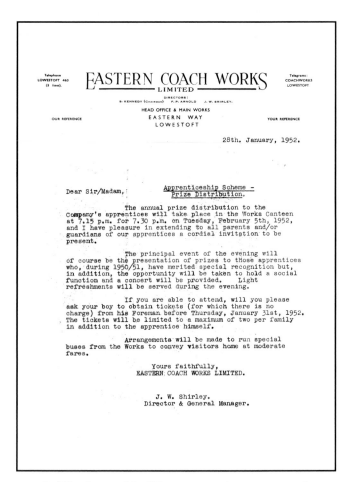

Irthlingborough's life was coming to an end as production capacity was increased at Lowestoft and the L chassis was being phased out. It seems not to have been handled too well for a letter in *The Hooter* revealed a lack

Bill Shirley, seen front row centre, arranged to be photographed with some of his colleagues before he left for Park Royal in 1953.
Shown below in numerical order they were:

1	Ronnie Statham, Development Engineer	13	Cyril Jackson, Chief Draughtsman
2	Tom Chaplin, Saw Mill Foreman	14	Frank George, Fitters Shop Foreman
3	Ernie Woolner, Panel Shop Foreman	15	Jack Baldwin, Trimmers Shop Foreman
4	Claude Pearson, Finishing Shop Foreman	16	Percy Talman, Materials Controller
5	Gus Halkes, Assistant Chief Inspector	17	Frank Bayliss, Stores Officer
6	Ted Godley, Establishment Welfare Superintendent.	18	CM Woodburn, Company Secretary
7	Les Saunders, Body Shop Foreman	19	Alf Tattersall, Works Manager
8	Reg Salts, Paint Shop Foreman	20	Bill Shirley, Managing Director & General Manager
9	Albert McCall, Commercial Officer	21	Ralph Sugden, Assistant General Manager
10	Harrold Boddy, Chief Inspector	22	John Ross, Chief Designer
11	Jack Smith, Assistant Secretary	23	Jess Wright, Electrician's Foreman
12	Allen Swan, Assistant Stores Officer		

The versatility of the basic ECW body was demonstrated by its customers. Although this West Yorkshire Road Car Bristol L was built with a standard rear entrance, that has been sealed in this view, and a folding front door fitted by the operator for one-man-operation. The lack of opening windows is noteworthy, with a primitive form of forced ventilation fitted with louvres over the normal windows.

A promising hope was the loan of Bristol Tramways (as it then was) LS5G PHW 918 to London Transport for comparative trials in Green Line service. Finished in Lincoln Green with Roundel and lining out, it is seen here at Reigate. Although the chassis was fitted with Hobbs semi-automatic transmission to aid its cause, it did not find favour in what was probably by then a satiated market. Ironically the Coach Factory had to wait until 1985 for 'bulk' for London Transport – and this was to be its last ever, if biggest, order.

This picture is not out of date sequence for as late as 1957 Wilts and Dorset took a batch of LWL vehicles for rural routes, notwithstanding the number of LSs already in use. By 1960 the LWLs were virtually redundant and required rebuilding for one-man-operation if they were to be of continuing use. ECW did the first conversion, seen here, and the operator subsequent ones. Although doubtless attractive to someone, subtlety seems to have escaped the designer, and 'workman-like' is perhaps the kindest description of LAM 110.

of information, but in July 1952 it closed, having been the means of keeping the company alive in the crucial war years.

Writing in *The Hooter* Christmas 1952 issue Bill Shirley announced his satisfaction at the year's performance, stating that the change from wooden to aluminium body framing – by then complete – had not resulted in one redundancy. Although some short-time working had been necessary this had been due to non-availability of raw materials and the late delivery of chassis. More importantly, he also announced his forthcoming departure. In a separate article the Editor mentioned the continuing power cuts and, also, the shortage of scrap steel 'now that the big tidy-up had been completed in war-torn Germany.'

Thus at the end of February 1953 another major change of personnel took place when Bill Shirley duly left to take up the position of Managing Director of Park Royal Vehicles Ltd in London. He made it very clear that his years at ECW had been extremely happy ones and he was sorry to be leaving such a splendid factory. Ralph Sugden took his place as General Manager at Lowestoft.

Later in 1953 there were problems at far away Leyland Motors South Works where union pressure for improved conditions is believed to have been the reason behind the difficulties. Whatever the reasons the outcome was dramatic – in 1954 Leyland suddenly announced it would build no more bus bodies, and that its South Works would close almost immediately. Such was the speed of the closure that some operators apparently received partially-completed vehicles.

There are many who believe that some people within Leyland never forgot this episode and when confrontation or difficult market situations returned they played the tape over again. There are others who believe that Leyland may have engineered situations to provide such confrontation, though the cynics claimed that Leyland could never have engineered anything so far reaching. Whatever may be the truth we shall see this speedy closure tactic again but what a pity no one had the courage in later years to do it where it really needed doing, at Longbridge. Many of Leyland's problems which later affected ECW's position stemmed from having to pour money which should have been invested in the bus business into a bottomless pit of malcontented car assemblers.

Back at Lowestoft, production of the Lodekka meant that the double-deck output was now concentrated on one design, but the model was developed and from an open platform rear-entrance model it gradually evolved into a forward-entrance flat floor vehicle second to none.

The single-deck range, by contrast, expanded steadily. In November 1954 a prototype lightweight 35-seat single-

decker, the SC, made its appearance and only two months later it went into production.

One area where there had been investment in the factory was the grp or fibreglass department which had started off in the former RAF Nissan hut left on the sports field after the end of the war. Ronnie Statham put considerable effort into this project and such was the skill developed that two complete fibreglass-bodied SCs were produced, though that particular avenue was not pursued.

The capability of staff and material had been proven, however, and the department grew in size and importance. The grp content of the vehicles gradually increased and eventually the whole upper-deck first bay would be produced as a one-piece moulding. Domes and wings, together with a host of smaller components, were now produced by this new manufacturing technique and the role of the traditional metal workers with their panel beating skills was gradually phased out.

The department's workforce was classed as semi-skilled and some labourers were given the opportunity to improve their position. This was the start of de-skilling at Lowestoft but because it represented such a small proportion of the whole it was not seen as a threat.

By the end of the 'fifties L, K and SC production had finished though two other models, the SUS and SUL were following on from the SC. When the figures were checked an impressive 3,465 Ks had been built, though even this would be exceeded by the Lodekka which ran to 5,200 vehicles. There was a continuing pattern of developing vehicles to suit sections of the market and always making sure that Bristol and ECW could produce what the operating fleets required.

An order for two lightweight railbuses was placed by British Railways with Bristol and ECW built the bodies in

The completion of the one-thousandth Lodekka was seen as cause for celebration and a visit by the local photographer. Brian Ratcliffe, when interviewed in 1994, remarked with a wry smile that in all his 35 years with ECW it was the only time he could recall *anything* being celebrated at the factory! Over four thousand more Lodekkas would be built.

Bristol and ECW had produced several vehicles were recognised as leaders, and the Lodekka was undoubtedly one. It must have made a change to see a batch come out of the paintshops in a livery other than Tilling green or red. This FLF Lodekka for Mansfield & District was finished in the operator's smart blue colour scheme which was retained when the former Balfour Beatty operator was taken into the BTC empire. The other model would would undoubtedly have seen Bristol and ECW secure for many years was the RE family. Popular, well-engineered and in great demand its demise to eliminate competeition for the Leyland National single-decker was the final confirmation that no model, and therefore probably no factory, would be allowed to stand in the way of the Workington product. An RE bus is seen below.

1958. Seating 56 passengers they were part of an attempt to tackle the railways unprofitable rural routes and were sent to work in Scotland. The strategy was not successful and by 1966 most vehicles built for this experiment, including the two ECW examples, had been withdrawn.

John Ross, designer of the Lodekka, had become Chief Designer at Lowestoft by 1961, and the 'swinging sixties' were to see great changes in the industry. It is a sobering thought that at that time the average busman's take home pay, without overtime, was £10 per week. Men in the factory would be better off, particularly with bonus, but the

busman's wage was typical of the national average.

Further ramifications in the nationalised industry meant that the BTC was disbanded in 1962, and its shares passed to the Transport Holding Company. Another significant move occured when Leyland merged with ACV, to whom Park Royal, Roe and AEC belonged.

Of more direct interest in the factory at this time was the completion of the first RE vehicle, the rear-engined single-decker which would be so successful that in a few years time Leyland would have to kill it off to give its new and struggling single-decker any chance of survival.

Six

1965-1975 – Leyland comes in through the back door

The nationalisation of the railways and Tilling Group buses in 1948 has been mentioned, for it had a seriously adverse effect on ECW's potential sales outlets. Eventually the Bristol MP in whose constituency the BCV factory was located came up with a simple scheme to resolve the situation. In a financial manoeuvre in October 1965 Leyland, which had merged with ACV in 1962, exchanged shares in Park Royal to the equivalent value of 25% of ECW's shareholding. In one simple move Tony Benn had reopened the door to unrestricted sales opportunities.

Unfortunately he also let Leyland in at the same time, though he cannot be blamed for not forseeing that both his constituents and those of his opposite number Jim Prior, MP for Lowestoft, would all join the dole queue partly as a consequence of what appeared to a commendable strategy.

In 1965 both Bristol and Eastern Coach Works were in a strong position. Their products were well engineered and well respected and factory output and forward orders at Lowestoft gave an average production rate of between 650 and 700 vehicles per year for the next three years. The Tilling Group still controlled most production but the

Lodekka had a firm following in Scotland and the RE had strong sales potential.

In response to the rear engined Fleetline and Atlantean double-deck chassis introduced by Daimler and Leyland, Bristol had developed the VR model (originally intended to be designated the N-type) with rear engine, and Stan George – now in charge of double-deck design – had designed ECW's body for this chassis. It was to be the standard Tilling group double-decker and two prototypes were in the course of construction.

Once the share exchange had taken place both Bristol and ECW were able to go out looking for business from the non-Tilling companies and some broadening of the model range took place to accommodate the requirements of new or potential customers.

1966 was a momentous year for Bristol and ECW for the VR first appeared at the Commercial Motor Show of that year. VRX 001 (EX10) is seen here in the Finishing Shop, probably in August. The vehicle became a Bristol demonstrator, albeit outwardly appearing as Central SMT BN331, (GGM 431D). Some of the other ideas for this type – way ahead of their time, were probably doomed to failure as a result.

Outside Influences 1965-1970

An important factor for the bus industry's future, however, was the change of government, for in 1964 a Labour administration had been elected and Barbara Castle was appointed Transport Minister in December 1965. Her brief was to improve the image and effectiveness of public transport, and the effects were to be far reaching. Labour were re-elected in 1966 and the pace of change quickened.

Change was evident in other areas of life. The 'Golden Age' of bus travel had gone. The rapid increase in car ownership was one factor, watching television in the evening, instead of going out, was another. Television closed cinemas and, many believe, also started the decline in attendance at Sunday evening church services with the timing of the screening of *The Forsyte Saga*. Meanwhile, in the manufacturing side of the bus industry, Weymanns of Addlestone closed early in 1966 whilst Harringtons, quality coach builders from Hove, closed in May 1966. The following year Northern Counties in Wigan purchased local rivals Massey Brothers and in 1968 Duple moved production from London to the Blackpool factory which it had bought in 1960 – the industry was slimming down in a changing market.

A move to ease the problem of shortage of platform staff, and at the same time increase productivity, resulted in one-man-operation of double-deckers becoming legal in July 1966 and the future pattern of bus requirements changed overnight. If there were any doubts in the factory as to the viability of double-deck o-m-o, local General Manager J R Hanchett of Great Yarmouth dispelled them when he introduced it on July 1st, the very first day that it was possible.

In October of 1966 the Commercial Motor Show offered a variety of pointers to the future and amongst the more interesting vehicles were Daimler's 33ft Fleetline and two Bristol VRL demonstrators, the one on the ECW stand being finished in Central SMT colours as illustrated on the previous page. Clearly the double-decker was still seen by some as the front line product.

Leyland and London Transport, however, believed that the single-decker held the key to the future. The latter still forecast that demand for single-deckers would run at 3,000 units per year and showed Barbara Castle its prototype single-deck Commutabus in January 1967. What credence was place on these projections at Lowestoft is not recorded, but production continued unabated at the existing levels until 1970 and there was no cause for alarm.

Significantly the RE was now accounting for roughly 50% of all Lowestoft production, having been recognised as a very successful model throughout the industry, and orders were being obtained from BET companies, municipalities, major independents and PTEs, in addition to the core business from Tilling operators.

Meanwhile, in an attempt to strengthen the car making industry, the Government encouraged the merging of Austin, Morris and Jaguar into British Motor Holdings in December 1966 for it knew that in January 1967 the American Chrysler Corporation would buy the Rootes Group. Prime Minister Wilson had grave misgivings about the long-term security of the British car manufacturing industry, an industry upon which much of the country's economic activity depended.

With hindsight it is easy to say that in 1967 everyone should have recognised the problems ahead but at the time there were so many changes being made it was probably difficult to take an overall view. Harold Wilson was still worrying about the car makers and started to formulate his next move but it was actually Barbara Castle who made the next move. As part of the move to nationalisation she put such pressure on BET that, responding to what they saw as blackmail, they sold out to the state in 1967, allowing the creation of the National Bus Company from Tilling and BET in January 1969. Wilson, still worried about the car industry, lit his pipe and contemplated a merger of Leyland and British Motor Holdings.

If 1967 had been interesting 1968 was even more so. Ralph Bennett moved to London Transport and quickly proposed the introduction of one-man-operated double-deckers – which were proving successful in Manchester, the city he had just left. What Leyland thought about the effect on future orders from LTE – and elsewhere – for their new single-decker project is not recorded but they took the £10m government grant and quietly went away. Before the end of January they were back wanting more money, and also requiring the creation of better road access to Cumbria where the new facility was intended to be located.

In May, Wilson played his trump card, offering Leyland's Sir Donald Stokes a further £50m investment through the proposed merger between Leyland and BMH. What Stokes didn't know was that BMH was on the point of bankruptcy, and, with the assurance of Government investment for the new organisation, the deal went ahead. Wilson is regarded as having been the all-time super salesman in this deal, the sale of the biggest pup in history. Neil Armstrong's's famous walk on the moon probably took everyone's mind off bus matters a few weeks later, but the transport industry's problems back home had been made greater, not smaller.

Leyland was now able to plan to spend taxpayers money on its new single-deck project, and, meantimes, had been busy doing deals with government to create a new heavily jigged facility in far-away Cumbria where a completely new concept of British single-decker bus manufactory was to be created in an area of high unemployment. Leyland still believed that the industry would continue the swing to single-deckers and the new factory was planned to handle 40 vehicles per week, and with a semi-skilled workforce at that. Two-thousand single-decker buses a year was a very bold prediction, even for a company which had a monopoly of British chassis production.

Barbara Castle's Transport Act of 1968 came in October, along with the Commercial Motor Show which gave clear indications of city fleet preferences for the one-man double-decker. The critical parts of the Act for ECW would be the introduction of a Bus Grant equal to 25% of the value of new vehicles which met a specification to which the VRT and RE both conformed, and the formation of NBC, which should guarantee future Lowestoft orders, together with the formation of the PTEs which would almost certainly exclude many of the available orders. The Act certainly stimulated new business. ECW built 700 vehicles in 1969, 691 in 1970 and 938 in 1971, the latter being the highest ever total and one which was never to be matched.

Leyland's announcement of the FPB7 project and the associated agreement to create the Workington factory were made public in July 1969.

This, then, was the situation outside forces had created. What was happening back in the factory?

Changes at Lowestoft 1965-1970

In response to the new open market Alan Hunton joined ECW in 1967, working under Ralph Sugden, and found himself extremely busy following up tenders for municipal orders, something no one had had to do at Lowestoft since 1948. It may be significant that the post had not been advertised – Hunton had spent some time with Alusuisse and was testing the water when he approached ECW – and perhaps for that reason many people in the factory wrongly believed he was a Leyland appointee. Hunton had also been with Marshalls of Cambridge and one of his BET customers had been Ribble. Contact was re-established and REs were very soon to be seen operating in Preston. The good old days of Leyland's dominance had gone and just to remind them Harry Tennant, Ribble's chief engineer, made sure the REs were seen on service in Leyland everyday. Leyland were reported to have been stung and surprised, even they had not foreseen such immediate and damaging consequences of their 25% shareholding. Perhaps they had also underestimated the RE's potential.

Their reaction may have been more far reaching than was recognised. The realisation that they also were vulnerable in a changing market may well explain much of their attitude to their satellites, which now included AEC, Park Royal, Roe, Eastern Coach Works and Bristol, to name but a few. Doug Jack in *Beyond Reality* recalls that Leyland rarely, if ever, let work be taken away from the Leyland factories in Lancashire. A commendable attitude for those who lived and worked in Lancashire but scant comfort to MPs Benn and Prior when confronted at their surgeries by angry unemployed skilled men in years to come.

Leyland's influence at Lowestoft was minimal at first, and the feeling at Eastern Way must have been one of optimism by virtue of the bigger market place then available, especially as it now had its rear-engined double-decker almost ready. As 1967 progressed, however, more and more events took place which settled ECW's long-term fate. Back in Lancashire Leyland was pushing ahead with development of its new single-deck integral bus, convinced of the vast international market into which this vehicle would also fit.

ECW were pushing ahead with variants of existing models to suit new customers and to assist this a new drawing office was built. John Ross was in charge, as Chief designer, with Oliver Pease as section leader for double-

deckers and Stan George as section leader responsible for single-deckers. Lodekka production would cease in 1968 leaving only the VRLL and VRT type models to cater for double-deck business. Two-way contact with Bristol Commercial Vehicles continued on a regular basis and there was still a good relationship based on trust and a partnership of equals.

Bristol and ECW had resumed exhibiting at the 1966 Commercial Motor Show with the VR prototypes, and, in 1968, on ECW's stand, was a striking double-deck coach on the VRLL chassis for Standerwick, Ribble's coaching subsidiary, a BET flagship order even if by then set for inclusion in NBC.

Spring 1970 saw major changes within the factory following the sudden and unexpected death of Ralph Sugden who suffered a heart attack at Wrenton whilst driving home from a Tilling Board meeting in London. The following day Alf Tattersall was appointed to replace him as General Manager and Sid Wright was promoted to Works Manager.

The new men made little change, indeed with Tattersall at the helm there was going to be little opportunity. He ran the factory on a very tight rein, some would say a shoestring, and yet the results were there to see. Output rose, targets were met, relationships remained as cautious as ever and Tilling's profits remained very healthy. Stan George and Alan Hunton both confirm that this was an extremely profitable time for ECW, though investment continued to be at the existing extremely low levels. The era of the famous signs outside Tattersall's office had arrived, 'Wait' or 'Come in'. No one ever seemed to see the 'Come in' version, it was always a waiting game. Alf Tattersall was a master tactician and ran the factory as though he personally was paying the bills. Negotiations would always be after hours when he could be sure his adversaries would be tired after a hard day's work. Keep them waiting and then keep them standing up to retain the advantage were always his tactics but most people grudgingly admit he was reasonably fair, if somewhat sarcastic.

What was never questioned was his 100% loyalty to his workforce. His twin aims were to run the factory profitably and to keep men at work – and he achieved both. Remembered by Sid Wright with affection and frustration he would always consider that breakdowns and repairs should be capable of being rectified with a nail or two! He must have been concerned at changes in the industry and would have been aware of the implications of the share transfers whereby ECW shares had passed to Bus Manufacturers (Holdings) and then BM(H) shares had moved to be held jointly by NBC and Leyland.

As Leyland increased its influence so it began to attempt to impose its methods in the factory. The biggest problem, recalled with great bitterness by everyone, was the almost condescending attitude and the belief by Leyland that they were dealing with country bumpkins. The partnership of equals with Bristol was a thing of the past and it took many years for ECW people to put Leyland's arrogance behind them.

One example was in design and construction but

probably the greatest damage came from Personnel Managers. Len Webb had taken over the position of Labour Officer and Social Secretary at ECW from White, the Labour Officer, and Todd the Social Secretary, in 1958. He had seen at first hand how Tattersall ran everything efficiently and parsimoniously. He now saw Leyland introducing its systems into a factory which did not easily fit into pay scales, grading or methodology. Leyland did enormous damage with its attitude and severely eroded management's ability to control some aspects of the operation. They also took the profits under the new arrangements following the acquisition of all ECW's shareholding, needing these to prop up the ailing car business which Harold Wilson had 'sold' to Stokes.

Despite all these mounting problems production and profits remained high and men on the shop floor must have felt things were looking pretty good. Communications within the Leyland group, and the bus industry at large, were not sufficient to make them aware of the problems being created or experienced elsewhere.

'National' Implications

ECW's single-deck build was accounting for some 50% of factory output in the late 'sixties and this was due to the success of the RE models. Leyland's new single-decker, however, was designed to sweep the board and expected to account for sales of 2,000 - 3,000 units per year – a greater number than all then-current single-deck bus production in the UK. Those who studied the figures probably laughed and said Leyland had got it all wrong. So they had, but with a vast new factory in Cumbria to keep open there would have to be some sacrificial lambs before long.

In 1971 NBC had on order from ECW 650 single and 200 double-deckers. In days gone by Tilling would have placed virtually all coach business in-house but NBC was now using Duple, Plaxton and later to a less extent some continental coach manufacturers for its needs. Ken Batten was in charge of all NBC enquiries from the New Street Square head office, and his office was now also responsible for all material specifications and suppliers. With the Leyland influence there was no longer an automatic placement of orders with Bristol and ECW as would have previously been the case.

An increase in Bus Grant to 50% in 1971 gave the industry another fillip but in 1972 came the confirmation of the Leyland National implications. NBC ordered 498 of the new vehicles, to be followed by a further 520. Those vehicles represented three years single-deck ECW production, though less than 6 months capability at Workington.

The first of these vehicles was delivered to NBC headquarters for inspection in 1972 and since NBC was a shareholder in Workington it may be assumed that there was some satisfaction at the state of affairs. There must also have been concern, however, that even before this enormous facility came on stream the major city fleets had turned back to double-deckers.

In 1973 the Conservative Government decided to 'take on' the miners in a confrontation which left homes and factories in the dark and Premier Ted Heath out of office. The famous three-day-week will not be forgotten by those who experienced it, including ECW. Even Tattersall could not keep the workforce fully occupied and to crown it all Gardners decided to go on strike, thus cutting off the supply of engines. Workington gained from this situation since the National used a Leyland-built engine and production was not affected. ECW suffered through no fault of its own – a situation which would be repeated over the years as other external forces affected the factory.

ECW battled on through 1974 but in December of that year the company ceased to trade separately, being now just a part of Bus Manufacturers Ltd, in a move almost certainly carried out to disguise huge accumulated losses from Workington. Workington's problem was quite simple, it just didn't have enough orders. During 1975/76 it was busy and profitable – Doug Jack recalls that in the first five of its twenty years it built 35% of the plant's total output. In those same two years ECW really felt the draught and the realisation that orders were being placed for 500 Nationals each year for NBC did nothing to ease fears. ECW's main problem was that it was not its own master, and its former master had been emasculated. Political considerations would now come first and the huge investment at Workington could not be ignored by Government, especially a Labour Government partly responsible for its creation.

If the National was becoming a serious problem to ECW then equally the RE – a well-engineered and very popular model which was preferred in most fleets to the National – was certainly a very serious problem to Workington. Given the choice, which many operators still had, the RE would get the business. The answer when it came was frighteningly simple – kill off the RE. And that was just what Leyland did. Production was scaled down from 631 in 1971 to 65 in 1973 and 28 in 1975. Only the LH then remained as a single-deck product at Lowestoft and since it filled a niche the National could not initially cover it was safe, but its output could not save Lowestoft – 279 were built in 1975, 73 in 1977 and a mere 53 in 1979. Production ceased completely two years later. During 1975 – Workington's boom year – Marshalls pulled out of bus building, the National having taken away their market.

Leyland group finances were not helped by Workington's boom, however, being swamped by car losses. They recorded nett liabilities of £43m in 1974, and Lord Ryder was brought in to sort out the mess. In a desperate last throw he proposed nationalisation as the only way out, and the State duly became 95% owner of Leyland and all the problems. Local MP Jim Prior is on record as fighting for recognition by Ryder that there must be loyalty to ECW and its workforce, but the Workington problem was becoming so great that no one was able to stop its catastrophic influence throughout the industry.

What had seemed a series of remarkably good ideas in the early 'sixties were now turning sour and the chickens were coming home to roost – unfortunately they roosted in East Anglia.

Seven
The Final Decade 1976 - 1986

Nineteen-seventy-six was a watershed year for ECW for in that year Alf Tattersall finally decided he would take no more of Leyland's interference and took early retirement instead. Forty years of the various Yorkshiremen's reign ended on 30th April when Tattersall left.

He had worked hard for Tilling, and for Leyland, but he had no stomach for the latter's methods of running his factory. Reporting to regional office would have been bad enough for him, but to face interference would have been intolerable.

Several of his contemporaries, including Sid Wright, Len Webb and Gerald Vincent, each in different ways confirmed that the last straw was probably the introduction of Personnel Managers who effectively provided a by-pass round Tattersall in any shop floor negotiations. He felt he no longer had control and, in the circumstances, did the only thing he could by retiring. Whilst Leyland considered its options it invited David Cherry, Managing Director of Northern Counties of Wigan, to look the plant over. Cherry recalled that it was years behind his own factory in investment or capability and saw the problems of the Leyland connection. He kept some of his thoughts to himself but nothing came of his visit.

If Tattersall's departure marked the end of one era the arrival of his replacement – John Bloor – on 1st April 1976 certainly marked the beginning of another. Bloor was a Leyland man, but one who actually understood the bus business and, having been at Park Royal, also understood 'traditional' coachbuilding. By coincidence he too had been involved in aluminium airframe construction. Marcus Smith had confirmed the appointment and a new era of more open management arrived at Lowestoft.

John Bloor inherited a full order book, though the factory's peak of 938 vehicles in 1971 was just a memory. The RE was now almost extinct, and LH demand was far more limited. Though double-deck demand was good – 360 VR types was the highest double-decker output since 1963 – without the RE single-deck models the total volume was insufficient to keep the workforce fully occupied. With the end of Bus Grant in 1975 things could only get worse as the financial inducement to buy new vehicles disappeared.

Bloor recognised that for a variety of reasons, many due to Leyland's increasing influence, morale was low and that the long lead times were dangerous. He was determined to increase output and for the first time for decades serious investment took place. He took his message directly to the men in the shops, backed by convenor Ben Pitcher. Flow Line build was introduced together with an overhead gantry system throughout the bodyshop for moving sides

Sid Wright wishes Alf Tattersall, seen on the left, *bon voyage* after the latter's decision to take early retirement and leave the company which had been his life since 1938. Sid was to inherit the problem Alf was leaving – Leyland – and his health suffered as he battled for the workforce and its place in the industry. Though fully supported by his new boss, John Bloor, the task proved beyond either of them.

and fitting roofs. To provide improved manufacturing capability, side arm routers and multiple headed drilling machines were amongst the equipment installed. Sid Wright recalled that Bloor was enthusiastic and open to any suggestions which would increase productivity – he saw the first serious investment since he had joined the company in 1935!

Bloor recalls that following this change of policy there was increased enthusiasm on the shop floor as working methods came up-to-date and output increased and, without doubt, workers realised he was determined to improve things. He also recalled that the bonus system had stifled change and after long negotiations to try to introduce a better system he lost patience and imposed a system whereby everyone was paid a fixed sum for every double-decker that left the works, and 60% of that figure for every single-decker. The 'running sore', as Stan George later called the bonus, had been lanced and the cause of much bitterness between shops was finally eliminated. The problem between shops was always that the foreman in a small shop would find it easier to monitor the scheme, although the results depended on his acumen. In a large shop it was very difficult to make much money from the bonus no matter how astute the foremen might be. The unions, thwarted by Bloor's directness, always referred to this new arrangement as the 'Imposed Pay Scheme'.

The new equipment and the ability to produce components, allied to the change in payment system, meant that it became possible to manufacture items for the National single-decker and to supply these to Workington, which had no manufacturing capability. Interviews at Lowestoft reveal an irritation at the very fine tolerances involved, and the initial rejection of many items by ECW's own inspectors. What was not appreciated was the fact that there were no facilities or provision at Workington to make adjustments on the assembly line.

Although the profitability of ECW-built vehicles was good, and quality improved as morale improved, the politically motivated need to keep Workington busy continued to sap Lowestoft's strength. In 1977, the peak year in this period, 593 Nationals were supplied to NBC. This was another gloomy landmark of work lost from Lowestoft.

That year was a key one in another respect. Dissatisfaction with the situation at Leyland caused its Sales Director, Trevor Webster, to leave and defect to MCW. The industry was shocked and recognised that there were severe problems in Lancashire. Meanwhile Michael Edwardes was appointed Chairman of British Leyland and started to get to grips with the almost unbelievable anarchy in the car plants. It is not recorded if he ever visited Lowestoft or knew what or where it was.

An indication of the car-mania pervading Leyland's muddled thinking was the routine distribution of in-house communications which had to be collected from Nuffield Press Oxford for *simultaneous* distribution to all factories. As ever, the bright young men in Lancashire gave no thought to Lowestoft, and how far away it was. Bloor recalls these time-wasting trips to collect the material, each culminating in a session of paper aeroplane making back in the factory. Who wanted to know about Leyland's problems anyway? And if they did, wasn't it in the Daily Mail every day?

Bloor and Hunton now attempted to do some direct selling – with some success – but this was not helped by the lack of back-up material. Leyland was geared up to selling chassis, not bodies, although a brochure it produced eventually admitted 'Leyland build bodywork too' – what a pity they didn't remember that much earlier!

The Titan saga at Park Royal will be discussed as long as people remember the vehicle or the factory, but with hindsight a militant London workforce with weak management controlled by a muddled organisation determined to impose semi-skilled labour could have only one outcome. There are those who believe Leyland, having seen how easy it was to shut Park Royal, remembered the tactics for Lowestoft when the time came.

Leyland reorganised itself after the Ryder report which had led to nationalisation, but things got no better. Local MP Jim Prior, now Lord Prior, recognised the threat to his constituents and made strong representations to Ryder to safeguard ECW but to no avail. Leyland staggered on and a succession of Chairmen and Managing Directors came and went – most were hardly missed – but a body blow in 1979 was Marcus Smith's departure. Steeped in Bristol's traditions, and having been father of Leyland National since the beginning of manufacture, his move to LTE was another clear sign things were getting worse.

AEC's factory closed in 1979 and in that year Margaret Thatcher came to power. Her views on all state-owned industry was simple – get rid of it – and her determination to stamp out the huge losses later became almost obsessive. Meanwhile the recession began to bite and as unemployment rose the number of people using buses dropped, resulting in less demand for replacement vehicles.

Such demand as there was in the early 'eighties was tempered by another political scenario. Buses were to be deregulated and privatised, allowing a free-for-all to develop in Thatcher's market place. Neither she or Ridley, the arch instigator of the scheme, seemed to grasp that investment in new vehicles would halt until the situation settled down. That took until the early 'nineties and is still apt to falter. In that time even the mighty MCW organisation was forced out of bus building, whilst Plaxton took over Duple, Northern Counties went into receivership and Alexanders and East Lancashire Coachbuilders were both sold whilst in difficulties.

The last VRT, appropriately for Eastern Counties, former owner of the factory, awaits collection in October 1981. Building these had been like shelling peas, recalled John Bloor, and with orders stretching over two years ahead at one point the model gave tremendous security within the factory.

Eastern Coach Works had virtually no chance of survival now. It was a one-product factory building double-deckers for which there was to be little demand since the imminent privatisation had caused the National Bus Company to stop placing orders. The only real demand in the industry was for minibuses and Leyland would not allow it to enter that market, though if it had, only a fraction of the workforce would have been needed.

The unsuccessful attempt to bring the infamous Titan from Park Royal to Lowestoft has often been quoted as a reason for closure, but the declining market and the fact that the Titan was essentially a one-customer vehicle would have made little impact on the problems of keeping the factory busy in the long term. Whatever the merits or otherwise of the proposal, the additional labour would have been unskilled and, as at Park Royal, this was always going to be a sore point in a factory composed almost entirely of craftsmen. The influence of the national union organisers at the ECW meetings was interesting since they too were almost certainly more interested in keeping orders for Workington than for Lowestoft. It was presumably recognised that Workington's problems were greater than Lowestoft's.

In due course Leyland abandoned the Titan, though some 885 were assembled at Workington, and a less complicated vehicle replaced it. The Olympian underframe was produced at Bristol, now also suffering from Leylanditis, and ECW designed the body using Titan methodology. As the long run of VRTs came to an end there was a spell of utter chaos as the workforce adapted to the new design – against the clock of course.

The first production ECW Olympians were outshopped in 1981 and in addition to NBC orders vehicles were supplied to Merseyside PTE.

The Titan saga had left a sour taste in everyone's mouth, and relationships with Leyland continued to deteriorate. The next event was in many ways even more catastrophic and began whilst everyone was up to their eyes in teething problems with the first Olympians. Had they not been so distracted the problem may never have arisen.

National Bus had a need for a quantity of express coaches and had come up with the idea of rebodying earlier RE chassis which its constituents were operating. ECW took one of these and produced a styling exercise which made only minor changes to front and rear. The proposal was confined but just as everyone was about to get started Leyland stepped in. They had a large quantity of unsold Leopard chassis and no hope of selling them since the updated and improved

Tiger had been announced. In an apparently astute move they persuaded NBC, by very heavy discounting, that it would be better to take new chassis than bother with rebodying.

That decision was to cost Leyland and ECW dear but it must be recorded that the deficiencies in the body mounted onto the Leopard chassis were, as confirmed by Stan George, the responsibility of the coach works and not Leyland. The body design had been produced for the RE which had chassis extension members to support the rear of the body. NBC wanted a huge luggage boot and to achieve this the (optional) extension members were not fitted to the Leopards. There could be only one result and within days the first vehicles literally lost their luggage

By contrast with the VRT, opposite, the Olympian was a more difficult vehicle to build. Many of its features were alien to ECW practice and initially, after the delayed start due to difficulties in levelling chassis for fitment to the bodies, production was a nightmare – even with the investment which Bloor had been able to secure in better equipment. The DeMag hoist system can be seen supporting the partially completed roof in this illustration of a prototype in build.

A colourful line of Olympians outside the factory awaiting collection by their customers. The Merseyside examples, in their light green, brown and cream, stood out in more ways than one. In addition to electronic indicators they incorporated specially printed coving panels showing the Liverpool skyline, and also had externally mounted brown melamine strips fixed with Evostik between the window pillars, a real recipe for sticky finger marks! Later orders for Glagow's PTE had large areas of matt black paint and were similarly cursed by the finishers, for every finger mark showed and had to be cleaned off . Eventually, in desperation, matt varnish was applied.

boots and all they contained. The consternation increased when windscreens also started to drop out, the new design being bigger and heavier than the original glasses.

The cost of rectification was huge, but far worse was the damage done to ECW's reputation. Everyone closed ranks and even today most ECW people state, and probably believe, that the *design* was Leyland's, and so therefore was the problem. "Not so" said ECW's Chief Designer, "Under normal ECW practice there would have been a prototype and the opportunity to do full-scale trials. Building on the wrong chassis without time for a sample vehicle to be thoroughly tested *was* Leyland's doing, and they had to help sort out the consequences".

Once again relationships between Lancashire and East Anglia were soured and soon after Stan George retired John Bloor reached the end of his tether and resigned. There was sadness at his departure for he had been responsible for bringing the factory out of the dark ages of outdated manufacture, and had made many welcome changes in attitudes and applications. The export of Olympians to Greece had been largely through his efforts and although no serious business was obtained from overseas at least attempts had been made.

His successor was Peter Middleton and he inherited a no-win situation. Orders were insufficient to avoid redundancies and redundancies breed unrest. Building on the relationship with London Transport, where Marcus Smith still counted as an ally, he managed to secure some refurbishment work following the factory's biggest ever order – for 260 Olympians for the Capital. In an ironic twist careworn Routemasters were accompanied by, of all things, Titans and Nationals. Now the fitters could finally see where all those complicated panels went, but since ECW bodybuilders had the facility to make small adjustments at assembly stage the fitters would still not see the reason for the very tight tolerances.

Alan Hunton later recalled Middleton as being determined to do everything possible to improve matters, but with orders running at only a fraction of what was needed there could be only one outcome. The headcount continued to be reduced until there were less than 400 left and then came the final blow – Mrs Thatcher was desperate to sell off Leyland "at any price". An extremely favourable Management Buy Out was effected but the buyers specifically excluded ECW from the deal. Rover Group, owners of Leyland, had no wish to keep it and accordingly sent in their man to oversee closure. By Christmas 1986 it was virtually all over and an auction of what was left was held in May 1987.

Great consternation had been expressed on the effects closure would have on Lowestoft's economy. The workforce included many of the highest paid males in the town and over the last few years a procession of politicians, local and national, had attempted to assist. Eight years later it seems that most, if not all, of those who wanted to continue to work have found jobs and the town appears to reasonably prosperous.

In a parallel with Park Royal and other old established factories the long serving employees stood to gain a substantial windfall from redundancy payments and this must have influenced their thinking in any ballots.

And what is left? The factory has completely disappeared, but ECW-built buses continue to serve the town, and many others in the UK, whilst a variety of preserved ECW buses appear at rallies. A couple of small showcases in the Somerleyton museum give the only other clue as to the existence of the coach factory, though there are, of course, Venture's books describing the company and its importance to the local economy over the years on the shelves of the local booksellers. Otherwise it seems almost as though every trace has been eradicated, except in the proud memories of those who once worked at Eastern Way.

Eight

A Selection of Survivors

When ECW's designers advertised their products in the 'thirties and stressed that they were *built for long life* they didn't envisage the lives of their vehicles being extended this far for preservation of old vehicles was a rarity before the war and most vehicles which had been kept, as opposed to preserved, tended to be semi-derelict in the back of operator's garages. Fortunately a good selection of Lowestoft-built vehicles has survived but to the best of the publisher's knowledge none go back much further than these two. DDL50, above, is a Southern Vectis K, converted by the company to open top form in 1959, and relegated to use as a tree cutter ten years later. Another example from a slightly earlier batch is still used by the Company. The Westcliff example, AJN825, below, shows the original body styling, whilst beyond is an early post-war example from the Thames Valley fleet. Considerable work has been required on these and the other vehicles illustrated in this section to bring them up to such excellent condition.

The rear view of the United Bristol, above, shows the classic lines of the lowbridge K-type body, surely a masterpiece in styling. The basic outline, clean, uncluttered and yet so simple, would be instantly recognisable on the Lodekkas which replaced this design and to some extent on the upper-deck of the VRTs built some forty years after this design went into production. The United vehicle is a hybrid – the body has been transferred to this chassis from a Leyland Titan TD1 which had been rebodied around 1950. The length of the bays varied according to the chassis on which the body was to fitted.

Another example of a rebodied vehicle is this Leyland TD7 in the colours of Luton Corporation – the cab area was less happy with the higher radiator of the Leyland chassis than the Bristol PV2 design. Note the different design of sliding windows when compared with the Thames Valley example on the previous page. This vehicle has been restored by the present-day successor to one of its early owners – Luton and District, now known as The Shires. Sadly, with present British Bus policy towards company owned preserved vehicles, its future may be in doubt.

An example each of the lowbridge and highbridge versions of the body, both being to the 8ft width as built from 1948 after a change in Construction and Use legislation. The green lowbridge vehicle operated with United Counties whilst the red highbridge one was from the Brighton Hove & District fleet and has been re-acquired by its original owner; both are splendid examples of the model and are regular attenders at bus rallies. The United Counties vehicle is kept in the Irthligborough area by a local group, a pleasant association with the wartime factory though the vehicle was built at Lowestoft, of course.

The production version of the L single-decker first appeared from Irthlingborough, in 35-seat form, with an express version seating 31 following soon afterwards. In 1950 the model was lengthened, becoming the LL, and widened, becoming LWL, as the regulations were amended, then becoming a 39-seat vehicle. An instant guide to the LWL model on the actual vehicles can be seen in the space between the destination box and roof beading, present only on the wider model. The Durham District example, facing page upper, is to the original specification, whilst an express version to the revised dimensions and supplied to United Counties is seen facing page lower. The Thames Valley examples on this page show an LL 39-seat bus version at Toddington, part way through its restoration, and an LWL at Southampton. Note the later T-type desination display of the latter.

Royal Blue coaches for many years had a distinctive roof-mounted luggage locker with access via an externally mounted step arrangement. This LS6G is to the later pattern, without quarter lights at the front and with outward hinged door, is a regular rally attendee.

In 1965 ECW had virtually lost its way in production and to match orders with the build programme it was agreed with the operating companies that the 1964/5 programmes would be merged and full coaches omitted from the latter. Bristol Omnibus had an urgent need for coaches and this was met by a small batch of bus shells fitted to a higher-than-normal standard. These fitments included forced draught ventilation (with fixed windows) for which the grilles can be seen at the dome, seats and internal trim to coach standards, single-line destination box and Greyhound livery. Later they were downgraded but always betrayed their original appearance. This example personifies the type.

Two very different approaches to the requirement for a small bus for rural services. London Transport worked with ECW to develop the 26-seat GS class – Guy Special – using off-the-shelf components produced for Ford to construct the front end, and having a body which mimicked the RF design on its underfloor engined AEC single-deck fleet. The result was, in true London style, well-engineered, attractive and expensive. Nevertheless, if the vehicles had remained in service for a few years longer, they would have offered a sharp contrast to the uncomfortable panel van conversions when the bread van revolution hit the streets. In contrast the Bristol SC, a 35-seat model, was developed quickly and produced as a low cost vehicle. It incorporated axles from the popular Bedford SB chassis and used a Gardner 4-cylinder engine capable of returning in excess of 20mpg. The body design was later used when ECW rebodied some Ls and LLs as a means of converting them to be suitable for one-man-operation. Crosville amassed quite a fleet of SCs between 1957 and 1961 and two were still in service with Crosville Wales in 1994 – one extensively renovated by Crosville Motor Services in 1982 and another repurchased from preservation in 1989. In 1995, however, British Bus policy has seen one sold to continue its genteel retirement in Sheffield. The other seems less fortunate and still awaits a buyer in accident-damaged condition.

The Lodekka was a revolutionary concept that changed the habits of a quarter of a century – no longer was it a case of 'duck or grouse' in the lowbridge side-gangway vehicles. The prototypes had twin transmission, with the lower-deck gangway running between the prop-shafts, but the system was heavy on fuel. Production models retained the low height but with offset transmission. During its life the model was extended to 31ft 6in long and the entrance moved from rear to forward position though some forward-entrance models were produced to 27ft 6in dimensions. Open-top versions were produced for seaside operators. Crosville's DFG 157 seen above includes the Cave-Brown-Cave heating system with its distinctive air intakes, though the radiator blind is incorrect being a post-preservation addition as no conventional radiator was fitted to this variant.

The Southern Vectis model, opposite page top, shows the distinctive rear window arrangement of early examples. It was an open-top conversion in later life by the company, not one of the factory-built versions which were convertible open-toppers. Several of these have been recovered by Southern Vectis and are now in service again. The Southern National example, below, is one of the earliest production versions of this chassis and was unusual in retaining three-piece destination blinds at front and rear. Internally the 1960 batches were quite different from succeeding years, even down to having two bell pushes at the stair head for obscure reasons.

The replacement programme for the huge fleet of London Transport's RT class was watched with interest in the bus world. Traditional suppliers Park Royal and Metro Cammell would obviously be in the running but there was keen anticipation when one of the prototype Routemasters was scheduled to be built at Lowestoft. Unfortunately it turned out to be a one-off as far as ECW was concerned. The Leyland-engined coach version is seen here in sylvan Surrey during an enthusiasts weekend in 1995 whilst still owned by successor to the LT Country Department and LCBS, London and Country. The vehicle seems to have a reasonable amount of tendered heritage tourism work to perform and so it may survive the British Bus purge of such splendid artefacts.

Colchester was one of the municipalities to take the RE bus and this example shows the clean lines of the model. The RE became very popular with fleet engineers, its rugged simplicity ensuring reliability and good availability. There was a wider market than Bristol and ECW had been able to contact, until the shareholding arrangement which allowed free access to the whole market post 1965. Unfortunately just when the benefits of this wider market were being felt Leyland decided that the RE posed too great a threat to the Cumbrian upstart – the National – and the RE was withdrawn from the market, with the exception of Ulsterbus who had sufficient clout to force Leyland to continue supplying them, and New Zealand as an export customer.

Some vehicles survive because their pedigree makes them worthy of saving, but not always by enthusiasts. Northern Bus are major users of Bristol ECW products and in amongst the mundane can be found some examples of the more interesting. This vehicle was built for Southern Vectis in 1972 and represents the updated coach body of that year and the frame upon which the B51 was based. This particular vehicle has led a charmed life, for many years not even leaving the Isle of Wight. Consequently it is in excellent structural condition and the epithet 'for its year' is quite out of place. The vehicle will eventually join Northern Bus 'Heritage Fleet' which has several significant ECW bodied examples within its ranks.

The B51 cannot yet be classed alongside the vehicle above although, sooner rather than later, the B51 will merit inclusion in the preserved ranks. Northern Bus has several which are gradually being rebuilt with additional structural members to overcome their weaknesses. In this form they represent a workmanlike service coach for a few more years, especially on the few Tiger chassis thus bodied. Notice how much the nut rings on the front axle lift the appearance. Later variants will have an improved front although the ability to return one to standard will be retained.

Another operator with an eye for the unusual is OK Motors and its fleet includes a very rare animal, the only Tiger with a rear engine which Leyland produced, whilst the approaching storm clouds reminded observers at Gateshead of ECW's final months. The vehicle was purchased in semi-finished condition after ECW was closed and illustrated many non-standard features in its body. Clearly it was an attempt to build down to a price for the overseas market, believed to have been Singapore in this instance. A considerable amount of work was needed to bring the vehicle up to scratch but it is now a valued unit in this interesting fleet.

Above: The prototype VRT has already found its way into the Heritage Fleet of Northern Bus, although it still undertakes regular service work and is seen here at Dinnington Market Place. CPU 979G was new 26 years ago to Eastern National for its Southend-London services and the chassis appeared at the 1968 Earls Court Show. Perhaps the name Good King Henry would more appropriately belong to one of the convertible open-toppers of the fleet.

Below: An every day example of a working VRT showing how a fifteen-year old vehicle can look attractive in a good livery. This vehicle was new to Crosville Motor Services, passing to Crosville Wales upon the forced division of the Company. It was in fact the 5,000th vehicle to be owned by CMS. It passed directly to Northern Bus in 1994 and has been fully refurbished thoughout to demonstrate that the type can have a long term future.

Nine   A Colour Cavalcade

A union of equals: The badge proudly worn by Bristol MW types showing the names of the sister companies. The views on the next few pages show many typical and other not so typical ECW bodied vehicles. The authors may be forgiven if they appear in apparently random order, this is not intended to be the case, merely to reflect a small part of the diversity achieved by Series 2 bodies – despite an apparently rigid background.

In the beginning came the L type post-war body. JHN 384 is an L5G owned by United's subsidiary Durham District Services. The vehicle is standing in Waddington Street in Durham City, near to the local United Garage, bound for Easington Lane.

The early 'fifties produced some oddities and these Leyland Royal Tigers were high on the list. RHN 764 started life as United LU2 in 1953 but quite ironically was passed back to its originally intended owner, Cumberland, some years later as number 163.

The body fitted to United's Royal Tiger buses was virtually that of the LS. The standard product is seen here in the fleet of Jones of Aberbeeg. Jones was one of the first acquisitions of the newly formed National Bus Company and was put under Red and White (whose vehicle this was) for a while for management purposes. Amongst the first Tilling standards to be taken by Red and White was MAX 120. Notice that it has its fuel and water fillers on the nearside.

Another LS: This one is a coach-bodied vehicle delivered to Scottish Omnibuses and seen it the livery of its successor, in name, Eastern Scottish. The not-unattractive destination box was a later fitment when the vehicle was converted for one-man-operation as a service coach. The vehicle is also fitted with typical ECW coach seats, the frames for which were made from hard wood within the plant prior to upholstering in-house. To this day they remain one of the best designed and robust fixed seats for a coach – they make the seats specified by Leyland for the B51 appear what they were – miserable.

One of the 'Queen Marys' supplied originally to Tillings Travel, MXB 742 was a Bristol LL6G with 24-seat body. Later upseated and then transferred to Eastern National, this class of vehicle was always amongst the most comfortable of the day. Indeed James Crosland Taylor of Crosville described them as 'the most comfortable coach we have ever had' in his book *Crosville – State owned without Tears*. The batch also included some built on AEC Regal chassis and one of these starred in a BTC film about Coach Touring in the early 'fifties.

The problem of the rural areas seemed to dog the Tilling Group more than BET and was near irrelevant to most municipals who, by definition, were largely urban operators. In one of the number of attempts to resolve this, vehicle-wise, Bristol and ECW produced a number of lightweight vehicles, of which the SC was the first and probably least refined. Noisy and slow, it would still climb most hills, growling as it went, yet returning a fuel consumption in the 'twenties ! 6572 NG of Eastern Counties is seen leaving Surrey Street Garage in Norwich. Eastern Counties were traditionally quite inept in telling intending passengers where the bus might be expected to take them. 'Relief' seems a nice choice for a half-day outing – and a pleasant alternative from the usual 'Service'.

The contemporary heavy-duty single-deck was the Bristol MW which had succeeded the LS in 1957. After a short period with an 'odd' design of body, with virtually upright rear end and no waist mouldings, this attractive body was produced. Seen in United livery this former Crosville MW exhibits all of the original features of the body as it stands at Polam Lane in Darlington, prior to entry into service. This site, which was United's traditional headquarters, was recently sold and a Safeway Supermarket now stands there.

The Lodekka was, sadly, never available to the private sector and although a few attempts to sell it to the Sheffield JOC are documented, its potential was not realised. Nonetheless Tilling companies were able to enjoy its fruits even if, towards the end, their own conservatism allowed the chassis specification to lag behind its contemporaries. One unusual occurrence was the transfer of several very early Lodekkas to the Northern General Group from Crosville when 17/18 years old. VFM 632 stands in Gateshead green with Northern fleetnames and the customary injunction about where to shop. The old joke that some, locally, thought that Binns was a place will not be repeated. Note the Crosville-made glass fibre front which destroys the elegance of the vehicle.

One of the rarest Lodekkas was the forward-entrance FSF, not produced after the 1962 orders were built. Indeed a subsequent requirement of Western National was met with 20 second-hand from the Bristol Omnibus fleet. Central SMT B144, DGM 444, was one of the breed. This vehicle 'shows' the missing upper relief band moulding absent on Scottish vehicles for most of the production.

Staying with the Lodekka theme for the next two views we see the rear of a typical FS, 683 AAM, of Wilts and Dorset. Its Tilling Red livery, and cream glazing gasket epitomise the elegance which ECW had by now achieved. This vehicle is also equipped with rear wheel embellishers and, more importantly for the passenger, a type of high back seat which provided a very high degree of comfort despite appearances.

The FLF was the mainstay of production in the 'sixties and this 1962 bus of Western National has cream glazing gasket but the earlier type of radiator grille, an unusual combination. Unfortunately many Tilling companies omitted the black lining out upon repaint and the appearance of the vehicle suffered marginally as a result.

A tribute to the Lodekka is its continuing use on the arduous continental tours of Top Deck Travel even today. 1955-built LD6G is seen here in Berlin in typical guise. The term arduous should be taken literally as some destinations include the Indian sub-continent.

This Lodekka has certainly lived a charmed existence. Having served with Crosville for many years it was converted into a driver trainer; then when Crosville was divided in 1989 it passed to North Western for continued use. However, in the winter of 1993/4 it was reconverted into a bus – and renovated to a very high, if strictly inaccurate, standard. It entered PSV service again in 1994. Quite how long it can expect to survive in this guise is questionable, as parent company British Bus has spent much of the last winter selling its subsidiaries' heritage and novelty vehicles.

Another use of Lodekkas has been in the United States. The qualification of course must be that only RED Lodekkas are acceptable as they are passed off as London buses. However, it is not unknown for a little ingenuity in the use of the paint tin to be employed in advance of the buyer's visitation ! This conversion was a comparatively simple modification in the UK, with the door moved to the 'wrong' side and an extra staircase to the rear – the American equivalent of the 'C and U' regulations not really being able to cope with 'deckers. This was an E-registered vehicle from the (then) green Hants and Dorset fleet.

Thoughts of the London Bus demonstrate one area where the products of the coach factory were seldom seen – apart from visiting provincial vehicles. There were exceptions, apart from the final Olympians, and this Hants and Dorset K type HLJ 44 was one of a substantial quantity which were 'loaned' to LTE prior to delivery to their rightful owners by the British Transport Commission which oversaw both the Tilling Group and LTE at that time. In fairness this is a preserved vehicle but the LT roundel, destination blinds and the absence of fleet name but inclusion of the number, accurately recall the condition of the loaned vehicles.

Apart from the GS class vehicles and RMC4 LTE did take some ECW bodies on AEC Regal (RF) type chassis for its tours and Private Hire fleet. RFW 14 has survived and represents a handsome member of the ranks of preserved vehicles.

Another coach to serve in the London area was this B51-bodied Leyland Tiger which was obtained for Green Line use by NBC some years after the 'Country Department' of LT had passed to National Bus. TL 17 stands when virtually new at St Albans, in September 1982.

That largely was it for London until the 'contracting' era which has seen traditional London Transport services put out to open tender. One of the most successful bidders has been Ensign Citybus which is now Chinese owned. The requirement for VRTs was small and lasted only until more satisfactory lowheight vehicles could be obtained. This former PMT vehicle has, however, been fitted with typical LT style destination screens as well as the obligatory roundel.

And of course there were other companies and places that ECW bodies did not touch (or scarcely so). Of the companies the mighty Midland Red once built its own buses, but it did come-by four Daimler Fleetlines whose origins were with the Harper Brothers concern which was taken over as it fought to rebuild after partial divestment to WMPTE in 1971. TRE 949L wears Chaserider livery when seen here.

One of the places was Belfast and it was not until Ulsterbus/Citybus needed to take substantial quantities of Bristol REs to replace those lost in 'the troubles' that they were seen there. This is 787 OCK 344K, originally delivered to Ribble. A substantial quantity of these vehicles were themselves destroyed but a few survived to return to the mainland and indeed resumed service in another place where ECW bodies could not be said to have been natives – Sheffield.

One of the returnees was this former Crosville RELL6G with 53-seat bus body. The company responsible for these reimports was Northern Bus and the vehicle is seen here in an untypical Sheffield rural idyll, scarcely four miles from the heart of this once industrial City, prior to a major body overhaul at its new owners Central Works.

Northern Bus was not the first to base REs in the city as per chance South Yorkshire Passenger Transport Executive was grateful for the opportunity to borrow three from United Auto for three months in the winter of 1981. This was at a time when the Department of Transport had ruled over 120 of the PTE's vehicles too dangerous for public use. EHN 202J took the number 2018 and is seen on the City Clipper service – an operation which had up until then been accustomed to use by the UK's first experimental articulated buses.

The advent of the RE enabled many former customers of ECW to return to the fold. One of the best known for single-deckers in the post-war period was North Western Road Car. 382 (SJA 382K) was one of a large batch which was in the course of supply when the company was broken up and split amongst Crosville, SELNEC and Trent in 1972. Number 382 subsequently passed to Crosville and was quickly repainted green – probably by Ribble. It is seen here set to work on the joint Crosville/ North Western service 146 from Chester to Northwich.

The RE bus body appeared in three main guises, of course, and the intermediate one was that with the tall flat windscreen. As readers of these pages will recall, windscreens seemed to trouble ECW's designers and whilst this design solved the problem of taller drivers being unable to see the road, a cure for reflections had to wait until the BET screen was fitted about eighteen months later. RLE 868 of Eastern Counties is seen in NBC local coach livery and boasts dual-purpose bus seats – of a meagre sort – in its body. The Lincolnshire MW shown on page 108 epitomises the true ECW DP seat, this a poor substitute which appeared first in 1966 for Crosville amongst others. It is doubtful whether this compromising economy can be blamed upon Leyland – unlike most other criticisms over the next few years.

The RE soldiers on although its days are now surely numbered. The last survivor of PMT's once-large fleet it is seen here as a 'Customer Service Unit' – in which guise it is still used. Passengers are now known as 'customers' in many quarters but the unglamorous title 'Unit' seems to let the image down sharply.

The RE's small cousin, the Bristol LH, has had a chequered life – with only United Automobile clinging onto examples in even reasonable numbers now. Bristol Omnibus took a large quantity over several years but most of these were quickly dispersed when only a couple of years old. One which did not suffer this fate was DHW 293K which shows the unusual double headlights of its batch. The rear wall also incorporates a reversing window suitable for a contortionist. Another unusual feature – on the chassis – was semi-automatic transmission. The vehicle is still with only its second owner and is maintained to the highest standard. On this occasion it was proudly displayed at the Bristol rally in 1994.

Leyland might have developed a reasonable order load for the private sector had it wanted – the lure of a large order from NBC however made loading the plant easy – until the music stopped in 1984/5. One exception was this dual-purpose seated LHS supplied to Westerbus. It is seen here in Inverness Bus Station in its somewhat drab livery.

Scotland had traditionally generated a sizeable order load for the Coach Factory – until the Bristol VRT episode stopped this for a while. The entire fleet was dispersed, two to Osbournes of Tollesbury, one to a contractor as a workmen's bus (though still believed in service with the same firm today) and the rest to the National Bus Company. A few survive although this rarity, a 33ft VRT/LL, was converted to open-top by a group subsidiary. It has now found its way to Scarborough – where it was pictured in 1994.

Not all open-top VRTs were casualties of low bridges, or time-expired exiles. South Wales took three of the 50 built in 1977/8. Although now transferred within Badgerline, this example is seen here in a representation of its owner's traditional livery.

Another to 'lose its head' was this RE of Southern Vectis. This is the other such conversion and the quite pleasant lines can be seen. It also is still in service with its original owner.

Contrasting means of getting to the Isle of Wight. Although it would not have been possible to use either of these two to ride like the open RE pictured above, these two downgraded 1962 MW coaches of Hants and Dorset were providing land transport for the Hydrofoil and the British Rail Hovercraft respectively. Although economically down-graded for a long life, the indicator box in this instance could perhaps be best described as 'a monstrous carbuncle on the side of a dear old friend !' – with due acknowledgments to HRH The Prince of Wales.

Over the years ECW inevitably produced a number of prototypes – indeed many are illustrated in these pages. Still to be found in the Eastern Transport Collection is this prototype LS – MAH 744. It remains the property of FirstBus subsidiary Eastern Counties and has been reasonably restored to a likeness of its original form. Quite unbelievably the other prototype, NHU 2, also survives – being in private preservation at the Dewsbury Bus Museum in Yorkshire.

The most famous prototypes would certainly have been the two REs, 7431 HN (REX001, the bus) and 521 ABL (REX002, the coach). Sadly neither survives, the bus having 'disappeared' and the coach scrapped because no-one had the £1800 to secure it in the mid-'seventies. Oh dear ! Number 7431 HN is seen here in a rare view outside the Coach Factory, probably in the winter of 1962/3 when it returned for modifications. Certainly it is not prior to delivery. At this time it still retains the deep windscreens which were unique to it. In what is unfortunately a poor view, 521 ABL is seen, below, in service with Oxford South Midland, around 1970, after it had been fitted with electrically-operated doors for one-man-operation.

A stillborn effort to promote CKD assembly was the ECW-bodied C27 National underframe. It was not fully fitted out and disappeared from public notoriety for a while. Always believed with Traveller this 1994 view at the garage of Fishwick's at Leyland proves the point. The Preston office issued 'W' registration suggests disposal by Leyland Bus C1980.

The B51 era was heralded by the 1982 rebuild of Eastern National VHK 177L, a Bristol RELH6G. The vehicle is still in front line service today, registered 929 CVJ, operating with Northern Bus and is seen here in June 1995 in a new Commuter Express livery.

The less satisfactory side of the B51 was the cheapened form in which it appeared on Leyland mid-engined chassis. The sad tale is told elsewhere in this volume but here, in a mood of some optimism at the preparation of a new product, is United Counties CNH 170X, the first, undergoing its tilt test at the factory.

The Olympian was the only product of any substance in the final years and it is seen here in standard NBC form in service with Northern General Transport – nowadays divided into several subsidiaries and itself called The Go Ahead Group. This vehicle demonstrates the dual-purpose seats, common in the 'eighties, as operators tried to improve the attractiveness of their product.

Two further Olympians were built, both of which owed quite a lot to local styling input. Both succeeded in their own way. The first was this 11-metre body for commuter coaches for National Bus subsidiaries in the London area. These were highly sought after at the time when the old Southern region of British Rail was at its nadir and people were certainly talking with their bottoms ! – onto coach seats. Chris Green was, however, moved within British Rail to take control of a newly-formed Network South East. His efforts were certainly successful and the boom ended as quickly as it had started. Consequently, many of these lumbering giants were dispersed to a host of vaguely suitable provincial uses. Whether or not the Privatisation of British Rail revives this type of service, it is unlikely that these vehicles will be on hand to share in it.

Another effort to sustain the plant was the half-hearted sales into Hong Kong and the Far East. Seen in China, this vehicle is one of the later two 14ft 2in high vehicles which went to Hong Kong Citybus. Unfortunately their singularity is their downfall and the first vehicle (the lower 13ft 8in prototype) is already relegated to being the world's best Driver Training Bus !

One of the ambassadors for the plant was the ex-Lothian Olympian pictured in a cream livery in the last volume. It eventually found its way into the Citybus fleet in Hong Kong where it resides today. Notice that it has gained an Alexander front lower windscreen.

Now you know

Has anyone ever wondered quite how the blinds were fitted into the early post-war L type body ? Here's how. This is the second style, of course, where the three-track number blind layout has been introduced to make setting displays easier, to economise on linen by enabling shorter blinds to be used, and also, as mentioned elsewhere, reducing wear-and-tear on the mechanism. The via blinds would eventually be phased out when the T layout was adopted.

And another one

There are two commonly used ways of removing the roof of a convertible 'decker: the first uses a hoist in the roof of a convenient building, the other a small mobile crane. Either method seems to produce that human vice of walking past unseeingly, as Andy Taylor, then the driver of Sheffield Wednesday Football Club's Team Coach, does. The top removal was in the hope of carrying the FA Cup around Sheffield in triumph. This is one of the traditional uses of inland open-toppers but sadly 628 HFM had to make do with just the team, as Arsenal won that year !

How better to end this section than the bitter sweet day when the last NBC VRT was handed over to local operator Eastern Counties. VEX 294X is seen on the forecourt at Eastern Way in the company of Sid Wright (Works Manager, ECW), Ken Polson (Chief Engineer, ECOC), John Bloor (Plant Director, ECW) and Bernard Rootham (General Manager, ECOC). Apart from the bus, which, fittingly, still works out of Lowestoft garage, Ken Polson is the only one of this group to still be in post today. Sadly, Sid Wright died as this book was being completed but the enthgusiasm which he and John Bloor had for Eastern Coach Works was evident in all the dealings which the authors had with them.

Ten

My Lord and Master

General Managers *		Works Managers *	
William Bramham	1.7.36 – 7.7.48	Alfred Cladish	1.7.36 – ? 38
William Shirley	13.5.48 – 28.2.53.	William Shirley	? 38 – 12.5.48
Ralph E Sugden	1.3.53 – 22.5.70 (dec'd)	Joseph Rodhouse	13.5. 48 – ? 50
Alfred Tattersall	23.5.70 – 30.4.76	Alfred Tattersall	? 50 – 22.5.70
John Bloor	1.5.76 – 5.83.	Sydney Wright	23.5.70 – 1981
Peter Middleton	5.83.-5.86.	Alan Hunton	1981-30.1.87
Michael Sheehan	5.86 – 1989 #		

Notes

* General Managers were always appointed to the Company Board during theirstewardship thus actually styling themselves 'Director and General Manager'. From first January 1975 consequent upon the cessation of the Company trading status, the post was redesignated 'Plant Director'. In practice this meant little as there was no Directorship in the normally used sense.

Similarly Works Managers were redesignated Factory Managers at the same time to reflect Austin Morris car division customs now prevalent.

#Michael Sheehan remained at Lowestoft until 1989 in charge of the closure and site clearance activity.

ECW was fortunate over the years to have both a very stable senior management team and the ability to promote from within. Bill Bramham was the General Manager from 1936 until he left to go to Northern Coachbuilders in 1948. Bramham was an Engineer by training undertaken at Charles H. Roe in Leeds rising to be Works Manager in 1926. Although he brought ideas and contacts from that Company to Lowestoft his was the name that appeared on the crucial bodywork patents in the war years. Fifty years later it is very difficult to say exactly what contribution he made to the ideas that were patented. However given that in many ways they reflect a continuation of ideas to be found in embryonic or developing form on Roe vehicles it is likely that he was in the forefront of development works at the Irthlingborough plant. It is believed he left over the impending nationalisation of his company, his career subsequently taking him to Northern Coachbuilders in Newcastle and later Saunders Roe at Beaumaris on the island of Ynys Mon when NCB ceased body building. Bramham was succeeded by his works manager of ten years, J. W. Shirley.

Bill Shirley had been educated in Birmingham and his craft training was at MCCW's coach works. During his time there he was involved in that concern's first all metal body and subsequently transferred to the Weymann plant at Addlestone. It is no coincidence that he was involved in Weymann's first steel bodies as well. He then came to Eastern Counties Omnibus Co as foreman of the fitting out department. His experience in steel construction at MCCW led to his recruitment to the Leyland South Works body plant. Here his former boss Colin Bailey was working wonders getting Leyland out of the problems created by its first steel framed bodies. Bailey had been head-hunted by Spurrier for this crucial task. Shirley must have become aware of the problems of steel framed bodies at this time and the experience seems likely to have influenced his later career. Three years later saw his ambition lead him to apply for, and achieve, the post of Works Manager at Lowestoft, in 1938. When Bramham left he succeeded him as director and General Manager. He again moved on in 1953, this time to a similar appointment at Park Royal Vehicles. This was to be his last appointment but in the 'sixties a young man called John Bloor was appointed his Chief Designer. Bloor later became Plant Director at ECW bringing the wheel full circle.

A slight change in direction brought Shirley's successor from the ranks of ECW's Commercial Staff. Ralph Sugden was another Yorkshireman: He too had an engineering background and served at Charles Roe. He had joined ECW in 1938 in the stores and purchasing area, and was Chief Estimator when the aluminium body concept was being evaluated. Subsequently he was commercial manager and deputy general manager but with the advent of Nationalisation 'selling' – a minor discipline in some ways – was abandoned until the appointment of Alan Hunton from Marshall in 1967. The significance here was that the freedom to sell in the open market again demanded a technical sales representative. It was Sugden who appointed Hunton to this post. Hunton even today describes this as one of the best jobs of his career – he was a one man department and under ECW ways he was permitted to get on with the job. He was to achieve no small amount of success until Leyland ways were imposed. Yet despite twenty years at the plant up to its closure and being a native of East Anglia, he speaks of still being thought of as an incomer at the end.

Ralph Sugden died in office on 22nd May 1970 but was succeeded by yet another Yorkshireman Alfred Scholey Tattersall. He too had an impeccable coachbuilding background: Firstly at Charles Roberts in Sheffield and subsequently at Park Royal Vehicles. He joined the coach factory in 1938 as a section leader in the drawing office becoming in turn Chief Designer and Works Manager. Significantly he was at Irthlingborough during the war years. After twenty years as Works Manager he succeeded Sugden in 1970. He finally conceded defeat to the Leyland style of management and left the plant in 1976. He enjoyed

a deserved reputation as a coachbuilder and served the Tilling Group with some distinction. Always 'the boss' he had the confidence of his workforce and it is his demise that to many marked the decline in the coach factory's fortunes.

The appointment of John Bloor was a watershed in ECW's management. He was the first outsider to be appointed to top management since 1936, taking the position of Plant Director and more significantly the first true Leyland appointee to a senior position. The man passed over was Sydney Wright who continued for some years in the post of Factory Manager. Bloor in some ways represents a halfway house. Leyland Vehicles as an entity was at best suspicious of traditional coachbuilders, going back to the abrupt closure of Leyland Motors own body plant in the early 'fifties. Bloor started with a motor car background at Ford and subsequently the Rover Group which in the eyes of many was the essential qualification for building buses – they too carried passengers! He had, however, diversified his career into MCW via a short spell at Guy Motors and subsequently became Chief Body Engineer at Park Royal. His duties here involved responsibility for work at both Roe and Park Royal. It was at this time that early work on the Titan was being undertaken. In many ways he was the ideal candidate to replace Alf Tattersall. If he had to be both acceptable to the Leyland personnel fraternity and yet be able to comprehend the prevalent ways of his parent Company he had the right qualifications. He certainly fought for his new plant in the

William Bramham

Ralph Sugden

face of those at Leyland who tended to pretend that like C H Roe it did not exist. He can be credited with much of the modernisation and many of the early export successes to Athens and Hong Kong. However in his book *Beyond Reality* Doug Jack describes the chaotic way in which firstly, British Leyland International and subsequently the Finance Department combined to frustrate meaningful export sales endeavour. His appointment was terminated in April 1983.

A true Leyland man was to succeed him. Never really accepted at Lowestoft, Peter Middleton was another engineer although one with no coach building experience. His early career had seen him in the truck assembly area although he did play a part in establishing the then new Leyland Bus chassis assembly line at Farington when buses were divorced from trucks. He busied himself with bringing in refurbishment work in an endeavour to keep the factory open, but a combination of Leyland malaise or malevolence and national politics was to frustrate him. He left in the face of the inevitable in 1986 to further his career outside Leyland.

The final plant Director was to be Michael Sheehan. An Austin Morris person of some years service he was appointed by the Rover Group when that Company assumed control of the coach works after Ian McKinnon excluded it from his plans for Leyland Bus. His appointment was to be nothing more than one to see through the orderly wind down of the business to January 1987. He remained after that time to manage the disposal of the redundant assets of the plant, and subsequently the land itself. He did not take any role, given or assumed, in seeking to reverse the death sentence pronounced by Leyland Bus.

Many other people played quite important parts in the work of the Coach Factory over the years and it difficult to single out some without mention of all. However several men deserve particular recognition as they perhaps are responsible for the products that grace the streets today.

Sydney Wright joined the plant in Eastern Counties days in 1935 and had various jobs in the plant as an apprentice. Inevitably war service interrupted and he rose to be a Corporal Fitter working on aircraft frame repairs. More importantly from the coach works view he managed to get himself into a section dealing with the research and preparation of technical manuals and in particular repairs. It was at this time that his familiarity with aluminium structures grew. He was demobbed after VJ day with the rank of Sergeant and returned to Lowestoft, initially in the drawing office. He was fortunate to have been well thought of and made steady progress upwards. Of particular note was that interviews for his jobs were always at Tilling Headquarters and conducted by the Directors who were of course busmen and he was for many years Assistant Works Manager. Upon the death of Ralph Sugden he was appointed Works Manager to Tattersall, a post he held until he retired in 1981. Ordinarily he would have been expected to succeed to the general managership when Tattersall retired but Leyland broke the line of succession which had been so productive. Wright was a committed coach works

Bill Shirley

Alfred Tattersall

man over so many years and played a part behind the scenes in seeking to rescue the Titan deal. Sadly, to the end, he still saw this as failure which was partly down to him although the greater forces which were at work and described elsewhere in this book were surely predominant.

The other major post-'fifties influence was Stan George who was appointed to Eastern Counties by Cladish, then Works Manager, in 1935. He too served his apprenticeship in the plant and spent 1940-45 in the Royal Air Force on aluminium airframe work. Upon return to the factory he went into the drawing office and by the beginning of the 'fifties, he was section leader-single-decks. He was the designer responsible for the LS body and the aluminium extrusions introduced with it. Also to his credit, with a little help from Bristol were the integral Dennis-based single-decks for Eastern Counties. His boss at this time was John Ross who designed the Lodekka vehicles interpreting 'the look' and translating this into one of the most elegant half cabs of all time and solving the practicalities of the new layout. When Ross retired he became Chief Designer and can be credited with the VR body to join his long line of single-deckers. To him must also go the credit for the curved front REs and the subsequent proposal to use this design on the N types design sketches. He continued to occupy this position of influence until he took retirement from the Leyland regime in 1983.

Last but not least is Alan Hunton who served at the coach works from 1967 and was the Factory Manager from 1981 until its closure in 1987. Hunton joined the plant from Marshall of Cambridge to the newly created role of Technical Salesman. He was appointed to the post by Ralph Sugden. Hunton was never fully accepted at the coach works – although born in East Anglia and having worked in the area for most of his working life many in the factory thought he was a Leyland appointee. Hunton's job brought him into contact with many former ECW customers where he was able to tell people that the country's leading coachbuilder was back in the open market. One of his early successes was to capitalise on Ribble's urgent need to reduce expenditure on reframing steel based bodies. Harry Tennant, the Chief Engineer, was as much swayed by the strengths of the ECW product as the Bristol RE chassis when recommending that Ribble should break years of tradition and order this combination in 1967. Hunton's contribution to the coach works was represented by this and other sales over the next years as well as his stewardship of the plant later on.

Many other people served the Coach Factory with distinction over the years, from those in the pre-war days about whom so little is now known through to the many in later days but whose rightful mention in this volume is denied by space considerations.

John Bloor

Eleven The Customer reigns ?

For the majority of its life ECW enjoyed an enviable position not open to its peers – that of sharing common ownership with operating companies. Initially United Automobile Services then Eastern Counties, the Tilling group and finally, but with markedly lessening influence, the National Bus Company. The benefits of this – particularly in the 'fifties and 'sixties – came in two ways.

Firstly there could be a far closer working relationship with the engineers of the operating companies, both to consider developments to the product but more importantly if only to tame some of the excesses of the commercial processes. This is particularly important, for where a 'tendering' process is in place, the lowest possible price is the order of the day, demanding that corners be cut and specifications be pared – frequently to the detriment of the product. Although ECW, (and indeed sister chassis builder Bristol Commercial Vehicles) were run as arms length commercial concerns, the internal market governed pricing and, therefore, if a particular technical feature was seen as being necessary for the product the temptation to price-engineer was removed.

There was a very straight-forward structure to technical co-operation. Each month senior figures from the Coach Factory would meet with the Tilling Head Office Engineering Director and in rotation the Chief Engineers from the operating units. This system served the Company well into the 'sixties and indeed into NBC days. As a direct result it was in this period that the Company's already high reputation was sealed.

Wedgwood Benn

However, 1965 brought the 'Wedgewood Benn' agreement whereby 25% of ECW shares passed to Leyland Group control. This did not make much difference to technical management until the formation of the National Bus Company, and the subsequent increase in the Leyland

The principal features of an ECW body can be seen in this illustration of LS chassis 93001 in 1953, destined to become Southern Vectis 844 (JDL 43). The whole of the structure is in aluminium and the through waist and cantrails can be clearly seen. The single piece vertical pillars are attached to the inner stress panels. The heavy waist extrusion which first appeared on these vehicles is a key part of the design, combining the use of the earlier patents of the Bramham era. This 1950 design by Stan George which first appeared on the LS prototypes NHU 2 and MAH 744, was to remain standard until the end of ECW-designed production 32 years on. The chassis alongside is 93051 destined to become United Counties 456 with dual-door body.

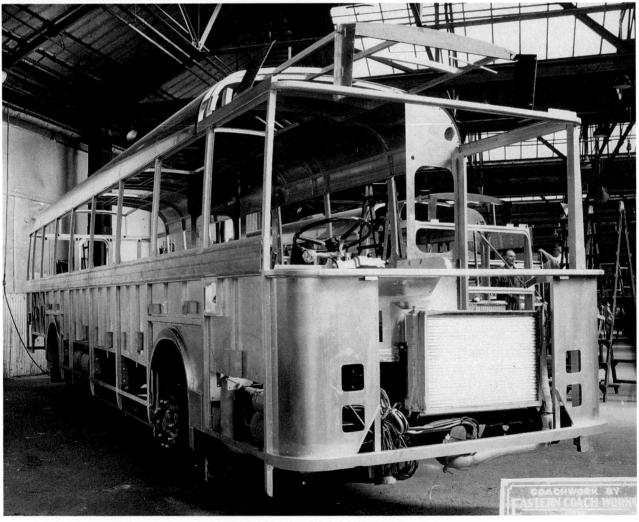

Group shareholding to 50%, with the even more significant rider that ECW was to be managed as an integral part of the Leyland Truck and Bus Group. Thereafter the line of promotion through which people such as Marcus Smith moved to and from the operating companies was terminated and, increasingly, all that was bad about the Leyland Group of the time manifested itself in ECW.

To trace the technical lineage of the product it is only necessary to look back to the immediate post-war period. The standard body styles created a family similarity oft commented upon.

Aluminium

The single most important step was in the selection of aluminium as the 'metal' for metal-framed bodies, standardised after 1948. The first volume batch of vehicles framed in this material were the 30ft LWLs for South Africa in 1947. This order was fortuitous in providing the impetus for the change, possibly the 'export' tag helping to secure supplies of this then-precious commodity in early post-war Britain.

The rationale behind the move entirely to aluminium framing appears likely to have come from Bramham who served with the Ministry of Aircraft Production at Short Brothers during the war. Other influences were undoubtedly the steel-framed Leyland bodies which were sent to Irthlingborough works for damage repairs during the war. What left an indelible mark on the minds of people there was the severe corrosion of the body structures found when the panels were removed. Leyland had quietly tried to recover these vehicles for rework at its own expense in the pre-war period but obviously this early attempt at what is now called a 'Campaign Recall' was not very successful.

People such as Stan George, who was to serve with distinction as Chief Designer until 1982, also served in the Royal Air Force during the war. His task there was the repair of aluminium air frames and so the material's benefits were well known to him. Interviews with employees who worked at Irthlingborough have proved tantalisingly incomplete. Those who would have been involved in research and development seem, unfortunately, to have died whilst the survivors were involved in repair work. Clearly, however, the talents of the top brass were not wasted and patents taken out by Bramham confirm what was happening. Whether or not Tilling Group was pulling the strings may be another matter. The research itself was completed during the war and, indeed, what became the standard Tilling post-war double-deck body was developed at Irthlingborough during the dark days of 1943, but the early post war shortage of materials and the need to produce as many new and rebodied vehicles as possible curtailed the innovation until the South African order produced the correct combination of circumstances.

Although others had 'tested the water', including Shorts in the late 'twenties, this total switch to aluminium was not taken by any other coach builder in the UK, with one principal exception, until the early 'seventies when Walter Alexander of Falkirk moved away from steel. Interestingly Alexanders had been part of the Scottish Bus Group empire of the same name but 'escaped' nationalisation when the operating activities were taken over by the British Transport Commission. Others doggedly persisted with steel for a further 20 years – the problems being reflected in the high in-service refurbishment costs of their products.

The one notable exception, Park Royal, became involved with aluminium – and looked upon it as its standard. Park Royal was no stranger to the use of jig assembled aluminium bodies, of course, having built hundreds of wartime bombers in this manner whilst under Beaverbrook's control as part of London Aircraft Production. Duple was also a part of that organisation but apparently continued with wood framing. Union intransigence may have been the reason – certainly as late as 1953 a change in working practices to build the Duple Roadmaster – using steel instead of wooden framing – led to a 37-week strike.

When Bill Shirley, ECW's General Manager, moved to Park Royal from Lowestoft in 1953, Bill Black had chosen precisely the right man to develop the London company's expertise. He took with him many ideas from Lowestoft as contemporary photographs of its products reveal. This interlude ended after some five years when the BET group demands for steel framing for lower cost and a planned shorter life were finally reasserted by S. G. (Peter) Vince the group's head of Technical Services.

The other influence at PRV was, of course, London Transport which placed experimental Routemaster orders with Weymann and ECW as well as Park Royal. The production orders all went to Park Royal, but this never influenced future production for the provinces where steel framing continued to be supplied. ECW did not take the full stride which might have been expected of them, however, and a not inconsiderable amount of wood was used in key parts of the product right up to the ill-fated B51 coach body of 1981/2. The wood used was teak, with varying grades according to purpose. Items such a windscreen pillars and the bearers for the ever-increasing numbers of flaps remained so formed. Quite apart from a weight penalty, rot and movement often set in quite prematurely, requiring avoidable remedial work.

Construction Technique

The aluminium bodies built for the Bristol K and L type chassis were the subject of extensive design work to develop a basic body frame using a limited number of extrusions to create maximum strength. That the research was successful cannot be doubted for the few vehicles that survive today exhibit no signs of body movement – not from ECW the drooping waist rails or splayed sides so common to many other manufacturers' products. This method of construction continued to be used for all double-deckers designed at Lowestoft, including the VRT. The cheaper rural designs such as the SC and LH were also built to this design (although the SU or Bedford VAM designs were exceptions). Although it is perhaps distressing to look at examples in action, the tragic accident at Wilberfoss in North Yorkshire in 1993 showed comparatively small deformation of the side structure of a VRT body despite an impact at a combined speed in excess of 60mph. Other photographs which exist and which show the results of accidents involving ECW bodies also confirm the strength of the structure with damage confined to the local area of impact.

Premium Single-Deckers

Similarly, much effort was put into the development of a new single-deck body structure for the Bristol LS and subsequent premium chassised vehicles. The LS was, of course, of semi-integral construction, in which the body structure provided much of the finished strength of the vehicle, thus prompting the development required.

The principal designer was Stan George, at that time in charge of single-deck body design. There was a very close liaison with the 'Motor Constructional [sic] Works' of the Bristol Tramways and Carriage Company. Leading for Bristol were two very familiar names – Cyril Eyles, for so long Chief Engineer, and Len Norman who was still head of the experimental shop at the time of the BCV closure in 1983. Every Bristol model from about 1950, and indeed all the prototype Olympians, were assembled under his guidance.

Many people looked at the moulding under the side windows and saw it as a slightly old fashioned decorative feature for liveries of the day. Yet it was this rail that was to contribute much of the structural integrity of the LS and later vehicles over the years. It is in fact a complex aluminium box-shaped extrusion with ribbed strengtheners, 3/16 to ¼ ins thick, running the length of the vehicle providing rigidity to the structure – and not insignificant sideways protection to the passenger compartment against deformation in an accident. This is a feature much talked of today by leading builders as if it were something newly discovered. Indeed the Cumberland Motor Services RE which crashed onto its side at Maryport in 1970 (250 – JAO 250 D) was found to be free of significant damage in this key area when eventually recovered. An externally flat form of the premium extrusion was developed for certain DP vehicles and coaches.

This method of construction fell into disuse when Leyland decreed that the RE body jigs and moulds be destroyed to prevent further competitive use in 1975. A consequence of the adoption of these icons of design was a useful spin off to the operator in that all frame extrusions were common to all vehicles from the K through to VRT. Sadly when Leyland took responsibility for basic design 35 years of experience were ignored with the obvious consequences.

The start was with the B51 coach whose story is told elsewhere in this book – although outwardly similar to the 1972 design RE coach the rail arrangements were different with catastrophic in-service failures the result. When the Olympian came to Lowestoft there was dismay and concern at the breaking of the waistrail at every upright, completely negating the in-built safety design which had been part of ECW (and all other bodybuilders) construction since vehicle building began. Everyone out of step but Leyland's engineers perhaps ?

Other Features

Keen eyed readers will also appreciate that the rubber glazing gasket was common to all vehicles in the same period. Although ECW made some concession to the appearance of its coaches, particularly the 1972 RE body when a Plaxton-type of gasket was adopted for the side windows, the section used was to crop up on vehicles fitted with BET windscreen including the Olympians built at Lowestoft. This simplicity is of enormous benefit to operators in both simplifying stores inventory and ensuring the variety of skill and specialist knowledge is restricted to one basic methodology.

The system of construction – for that is what it was – is as significant as that of Alusuisse. The latter has made considerable profits by licensing its system and selling extrusions. Its customers include, quite ironically, Optare

of Leeds, the successor to one-time Leyland stablemate Charles H. Roe. Similarly, the Volvo Bus Swedish bodybuilder Saffle is developing such an aluminium system today for the next generation of low-floor bodies. It is therefore worthy of thought that had the sales restrictions of the 1947 Act not been in place, ECW might have developed a rival business, in the 'fifties. Such was the novelty of so many of the construction techniques developed that no fewer than 5 patents were granted to the company in the period. These are tabulated on pages 138/9.

Glass Fibre

Innovation did not end with aluminium of course. As all manufacturers became caught in the operator-driven cost and weight cutting exercises of the 'fifties, again largely from the BET Group, glass-fibre became a new medium in bus and coachbuilding. In the mid-'fifties the first small 'glass fibre' shop was established in an old Nissen Hut on the Eastern Way site. It was here that pioneering work was completed to produce the more complex shapes to be found on PSV bodies both easily and cheaply. Two complete bodies were even built in 1959 on SC4LK chassis frames, although these were not perpetuated.

The two vehicles, which entered service with Eastern Counties and Crosville, led full lives although one drawback was that significant accident repairs to the pair always seemed to call for return to the coach works – presumably only one set of moulds existed. However the result of the exercise was to show that glass reinforced plastic (GRP) was not an economic material for full structures at that time.

As the 'sixties ended whole upper-deck end structures were being produced as were corners, valences and a host of internal fittings. Apart from the initial cost savings there was a further spin off to the operator. As so many of the panels made from GRP were in the vulnerable areas of the body, major cost savings in accident repairs followed. Operators began to see the versatility of the material, and they too established GRP Departments so that a great many other parts traditionally beaten by hand or produced on heavy presses were produced this way. Ironically ECW's Parts Department lost traditionally profitable sales because the in-house cost of the female mould required was minimal to a bus operator compared with the complex patterns used by the panel beater.

A direct side impact on this RE was sustained at about 30 mph on ice. Notice that the side rail, although deformed, has not moved sufficiently to even break the glass thus resulting in the avoidance of casualties. The other vehicle involved was also an ECW bodied RE which saw its driver's windscreen pillar and the front chassis member bent. It lived to tell the tale although the vehicle shown, 2173 (YFM 273L) was condemned solely on age grounds.

Engines to the rear

It was, however, in the 'sixties that bodybuilders' products were exposed to new and in some instances quite devastating stresses. Bristol and ECW led the way by introducing the rear-engined RE single-deck range in 1962, with United BR1 (7431 HN) and Thames Valley 867 (521 ABL). At this time there was one essential study which the designer needed to undertake, and for which very little 'experience' was available. The question was whether to mount the body 'flexibly' at the rear, so that the natural flexing of the chassis from the weight and movement of rear mounted engines was effectively insulated from the body, or to tie the two together rigidly.

ECW decided on the former course and, using its premium body structure, reaped the enormous benefits of both this break from traditional practice and the inherent strength of its body framing. The rearmost outrigger was nearly 5ft from the rear of the vehicle on all but one derivative of the standard body. ECW also had the benefit of progressive development, working alongside operators within the group, and this enabled some of the problems which did occur to be swiftly rectified with subsequent examples built modified to prevent recurrence. This was in stark contrast to some manufacturers where the customary theatricals ranged from denying any problem existed at all, through to demands by operators for compensation or else the threat of placing orders elsewhere noisily played out in the public arena. That approach led to the campaign recall and the destruction of reputations.

It must be stressed that ECW's personnel did not adopt that approach and product support to them implied support to the end of each vehicle's existence – however long that might be and whoever might be the final owner. It was yet another reminder that here was a coachbuilder which had been an operator – albeit many, many years ago – and the close relationship between builder and operator was a key feature in ECW's ability to satisfy its customers. Bristol's engineers, similarly, knew that ECW understood the needs of chassis manufacturers and the close working relationship was the strength of the association.

The RE body suffered from a few problems, certain of which manifested themselves relatively quickly, and others which only became apparent later on. It was on the Series 2 body with its longer front platform where difficulties initially arose. The lack of framework to support the deep roof dome quickly resulted in the latter splitting along its length. The lack of framing was compounded by the use of a combined wooden windscreen frame and corner pillars whose bolts tended to 'work' in the wood, permitting further movement. This latter problem was to trouble all ECW single-decked vehicles from then to the end of production, manifesting itself in moving windscreens and front end body structures in later life.

The then close liaison between coachworks and operator did mean that the cost of the product could be lowered where features previously designed-in could be usefully simplified in the light of experience. The most obvious example was the removable boot structure of early RE coach bodies, designed to assist in the removal of the rear mounted engine. Workshop practice across the THC Group developed a means of side removal using a trolley, rendering this feature redundant. The equivalent detachable panel on the bus body was not changed although many operators simply fitted a fixed plain panel during accident repairs.

Evolution

The evolution of materials to cheapen vehicle build costs was to become a feature of life in the Leyland era of the 'seventies, but some innovation was made in the 'sixties. For example 1in Douglas Fir tongue-and-grooved floor boards were displaced by ¾in marine plywood by 1970. The sheet material was treated with Oxylene by this time as a result of vehicle fires being experienced on the RE model. The cause of these fires was substantially due to the oily environment around the rear engine.

The sheet material had both advantages and disadvantages in construction. On the one hand the fumes given off during cutting were such that the operation had to take place outside the factory. On the other, during erection it could be offered to the vehicle much earlier, and without the delays caused by carpenters building an individual floor inside each part-built body over the course of two or three days. However, in service it was always prone to flexing and leaking – particularly as insufficient was known about mastic sealants in those days. Some quite serious wet rot could set in along the body walls and where floor panels abutted. It was always a curiosity that the low-floored RELLs and RESLs were more likely to suffer this problem than were the RELH dual-purpose or coach vehicles. In part, of course, this stemmed from the framing of the underfloor luggage lockers on the latter which additionally contributed greatly to the strength of the body.

The RE body was the last one to be produced under the traditional control of ECW. The complete vehicle gave as trouble-free a life as could be expected and the coachworks reputation was dealt no harm by its performance.

It was during the production of the RE series of bodies that the greatest and most obvious break (at least to the travelling public) with tradition took place. One possible downside which an almost incestuous relationship with the customer can bring is excessive conservatism. The interior of ECW vehicles remained essentially the same from 1947/8 to the 1968 programme. White painted ceiling, green (occasionally red or blue) rexine-covered side casings with only the upholstery likely to be different. The introduction of glass fibre moulding had meant that some parts were made in this material. By about 1962 pre-painted white ceiling panels came in, and this started to reduce the need for regular repainting to counteract act the inevitable nicotine staining when smoking was still a socially acceptable habit. The use of plastic covering – Formica- was avoided whilst others were starting to use it.

However two REs (for Crosville-body numbers 16471/2) of the 1967 programme, and their sister, the demonstrator LAE 770 E, were built using this material. The 1968 bus programme saw the wholesale adoption of 'Melaminium' casings using an attractively patterned cream base with a gold leaf leave pattern printed on (called Autumn Leaf, incidentally). Melaminium was a thin aluminium sheet on to which a melamine (sometimes called formica) finish was pre-sprayed: subsequently the material (often made to specific pre-determined sizes) was bonded to the walls of the bus. Metal areas were painted cream and by now the use of self-coloured GRP mouldings meant that these too no longer need be painted. White melaminium ceilings continued. The attractive green linoleum used by the coach factory started to give way to cork-based flooring materials, cheaper but not as durable, although the need to consider fire-retardant properties became important with a regrettable upsurge in vehicle fires associated with the inhospitable environment of the underfloor rear engine layout.

Even in the days of apparent standardisation ECW was producing variants to satisfy its customers. This FLF6G CSG46C was built for Scottish Omnibuses in 1965. Even a glance shows the unusual shaping to the panels over the door and the centrally placed front registration plate. This was only possible as the destination gear winders were placed inside the driver's cab. Other differences are the opening windows (or lack of), the subtle change in formation of the tip of the upper cream relief band, an unusual trafficator and modified rear panels (not shown in this view).

Leyland Days

The Bristol VR was introduced in its various forms from 1966 to 1970, and the early examples were built fully to the traditional ECW format. However by 1970 the Leyland Group had assumed management control, and that introduced a new generation of management not brought up in the ways of the craftsman. It also saw growing group influence over engineering and the introduction of cost-benefit analysis. Unfortunately the personnel policies of the day brought people in from the Austin Morris car division in the totally spurious belief that mass-production engineering was the answer to the building of bus bodies. In vain were voices raised in protest, whilst the profits from ECW's traditional output were sent back to go into the bottomless pit which these talented car makers had created at Longbridge. Had those profits been invested in Leyland Truck and Bus, where they should have been, we might still have had a British manufacturing capability north of Guildford, (and incidentally the profits sent back out in the reverse direction to the bottomless pit comprising the car divisions, not to local reinvestment where the money was being made).

Those were the days when engineering resource was being increasingly removed to Lancashire. It is strange that the three Leyland Group bus body builders were not allowed to create their own Engineering Centre, but it appears that the car technology used for the Leyland National integral bus, and the truck cab design team, plus increasing and possibly over use of computer-aided design and testing ruled this out. Practical experience and methods tested by simple old fashioned field use counted for nothing in the white heat of the technological years of the 'seventies.

The problems were undoubtedly compounded by an ingrained view of most Leyland personnel that people in the depths of East Anglia could not possibly know what they were doing, and needed to be trained in the basics of the professed craft. How wrong, and how much valuable time and profit was lost in destroying the country yokel myth. In summary, Leyland personnel adopted the 'not invented here' stance with a vengeance. ECW never forgot this arrogance. Neither did AEC, Daimler, Park Royal, Guy, Roe . . .

Car Influence

Throughout the 'seventies cost-benefit analysis techniques were imported from the car manufacturers, particularly as the American influence spread and certain individuals were starting to move from manufacturer to manufacturer. The emphasis at the coachworks moved from developing a product to meet the requirements of sister operating companies, to producing vehicles at the lowest possible initial cost (hopefully attracting minimum rework costs during the guarantee period) to contribute to Leyland Group fortunes. If, in the passing, a sound product resulted,

Throughout the 'fifties and 'sixties ECW continued its custom of many years in modifying the side mouldings of its standard coaches to suit United's retention of Orange Brother's livery layout.

Left: ECW often seemed to have problems with windscreen design as is described in these pages. Here a May 1963 mock-up of the revised MW coach front for 1964 can be seen in the Lowestoft yard alongside an actual 1962 design Royal Blue vehicle ready for delivery. The registration 1383 R was merely borrowed for the occasion from a vehicle under construction.

Below: The real thing! OWC 181 D was one of the Tilling fleet and is seen whilst working a Thomas Cook tour. Cook at the time was a state owned enterprise in the Transport Holding Company portfolio.

Another chapter in the windscreen story is represented by this recent view of two Northern General Atlanteans with the high driving position. MBR 442T on the right is as built but SUP 269 V clearly shows the operator inspired modification. Notice that the windscreen wipers have not been repositioned and one wonders whether the unswept area in front of the driver's eyes defeated the objective on a wet day. As only some of the operators of these vehicles undertook modifications and each to a different style, it may be assumed that the coachworks did not offer any retro fit package in support of this problem.

so much to the good but this no longer seemed to be the primary aim. This in turn tended to lead to Leyland style adversorial relationships with the National Bus Company engineers as future promotions brought in Leyland-trained people as distinct from ongoing internal promotion – no longer was there a common goal.

The manifestation of the new policy ranged from thinner materials, such as 18-gauge panels rather than 14 or 16, cheaper sealants, thinner fibreglass through to simpler constructional features. The influence was coming from technology which the Leyland Group then considered was satisfactory yet the passage of time has demonstrated this period to have encompassed their least competent cars ever. Concurrently a move away from price bargaining in an internal market to an arm's length relationship with National Bus – still a shareholder but now deemed to be just an important customer – also resulted. There was not inconsiderable pressure from various government bodies for such a move.

VR to decline

The VR body was the principal product at this time and whilst outwardly appearing to be unchanged, gradually suffered from cheapening materials. Wheel-boxes were made from thinner aluminium, and eventually they split or broke away from the body side. Thinner panels made unpleasant drumming sounds – and eventually commanded more anti-drum pads to prevent them too parting company with the bus. Another by-product of the thin panel was that it could not be used to exert the same pressure to squeeze out sealants into corners – endemic water ingress followed for the first time on an ECW product. Worse was to follow, and alternative methods of securing and keeping watertight the lower-deck floor structure in bodies on some Mark 2 VRTs and all Mark 3s caused expensive rectification and modification to be needed on many vehicles.

The VRT body cannot be described as a bad body *per se* – but equally certain quite unnecessary problems manifested themselves in ways not hitherto associated

The incursion of glass reinforced plastic (GRP) can be clearly seen in this view of a VRT destined to become Yorkshire Traction 903 (XAK 903T). The first bay of the upper-deck was a one-piece moulding, from roof to floor and from front to first window pillar. They were never difficult to find in the Lowsestoft stores when a customer required a replacement. Vehicles made the trip from the body shop to the finishing and painting shop right to the end of production. An Olympian is seen with its means of propulsion in the lower view.

with the coachworks. Indeed the modern syndrome of pretending it did not exist had been imported into Lowestoft in certain quarters by incomers. In many ways the loss of the close relationship between operator and both BCV and ECW was becoming a serious matter.

The most striking example of this came on the Mark 3 VRT with its sound deadening pack developed by Leyland Group engineering, leading to a need to remove permanently fixed panels from the ECW body to give access to the bolts retaining the ducting for the engine compartment air supply when seeking to change the gearbox. A makeshift compromise was reached where ECW cut some holes in the offside rear corner panel, and provided a cover to be rivetted back on. Such a thing would have been entirely unheard of twenty years earlier when there was proper liaison between chassis builder, body builder and operator, on the basis of each belonging to the same gentleman's club, with a common goal. It is ironic that Volvo Bus have made great play of modifications to their B6 chassis to obviate the premium which certain bodybuilders were charging to build on the model compared with the competing Dennis Dart. Twenty five years earlier with the RE and other models, Bristol had produced parts and layouts specifically to suit ECW methods and designs.

Coaching Sunset

It is sad that ECW will be remembered by many for the one product that was almost universally acclaimed for being wrong. This nadir was of course the B51 coach body. In 1981/2, in an endeavour to increase the product range, the Mark 2 body produced for the Bristol RELH coach was updated – or so it was said. This is not quite the whole story for politics intervened. The original intention was to perform a rebodying exercise for NBC, and the vehicle provided for the purpose was a Bristol RE, complete with chassis frame extension. In two fatal moves NBC and Leyland dealt themselves a no-win hand. Firstly NBC required a very large boot to be fitted, suitable for large volumes of luggage. Secondly, Leyland, by now up to its ears in unsold Leopard chassis, did a deal with NBC to take new Leopards at knock-down prices. No doubt they took the view that since the body order would remain unchanged they had been astute in moving the unwanted chassis.

Meanwhile, back at the coach works, the body had been designed to have a small boot with the chassis extension supporting the body.

The updating was done partially at Leyland and partially at the coach works – and the materials and certain methods used in its build were reassessed and their strength reduced to what appeared to be sufficient unto the day. Extensive use was made of fibre glass mouldings – often unsupported – and yet some either having to support heavy glass screens or alternately act as access traps for the engine. Major problems of movement were soon apparent. Further, to increase the boot size, even more of the rear chassis frame was cut off than normal on a Leopard, yet no recompense was made in strengthening elsewhere.

As stated the original concept of the body incorporated a smaller boot supported from the rearmost outriggers, and with a much stiffer side section with a proper waistrail.

ECW production was normally quite well managed but in this view one of the first three Maynes VRTs (VJA 667S) was ready before its seats. It was banished to the yard without its glass!

The B51 was a sad chapter in the life of the coach factory and one batch to be particularly afflicted was the BDF batch of 12-metre Tigers delivered to National Travel West. Three did hang on to their original bodies for a slightly more acceptable life and BDF 205Y represents the unhappy trio. As this book goes to press both BDF 204 and 5Y are being prepared for new bodies.

The original plan was to rebody some existing RE vehicles with the B51 body. One of the batch which was actually prepared was from the Eastern Counties fleet, its RE895 (SVF 985G).

The final insult was that the side flaps were so flimsy that the twisting combined with two or three years wear could cause them to fly open whilst the vehicle was in motion.

The actual responsibility for the fateful stress calculations for the cantilevered rear section lies quite clearly at the coach works door. It has long been the fashion to blame 'Leyland' for the troubles of the B51 – but that would be substantially wrong. The source for this information should, in the best journalistic traditions, remained swathed in rightful anonymity for at this time not only did the plant have to cope with the B51 but also the incoming Olympian body. This latter vehicle entailed new methods of construction and a total reorganisation of the plant and no small measure of variety even within the parameters of the new body. Technical and production personnel were stretched almost beyond reality.

The standard bus body, by 1980 reduced to be mounted on the LHS chassis, seemed to continue to look modern and the factory just missed out on the midibus boom. One of the last, GTX 760W for National Welsh, is seen in an official view. Sadly these ultra short LHSs were nasty little vehicles on wet greasy roads tending to turn around and return from whence they were coming under sharp but responsible braking. This led to mixed fortunes as can be imagined.

The product of any plant is an amalgam of talents from the most humble draughtsman at his first drawing board right up to the plant director and sadly the coach works made its most (and perhaps only) serious error at a time when it was at its weakest. From then on it was, unfortunately, downhill until eventual closure.

In build

In fairness to so many of the craftsmen at the coachworks it must be recorded that they clearly saw the problems even before the first vehicle was in build. Ray Durrant, the body shop foreman and others immediately noted that there were neither chassis extension pieces provided to support the boot nor holes drilled in the chassis to accept them. This chassis extension feature goes back to an Orange Coaches (London) patent of the 'thirties, to provide under-support for suspended boots, another example of tradition being based on sound experience.

The observations were duly reported upwards but the quick fire answer was that the design had been signed off and was accordingly correct. Just for good measure they were also told to remove a further section of the chassis members before starting work to increase the boot size. Whilst ECW had long had procedures which owed more

to the longevity of service of its staff and the traditions of the plant, the Leyland management could not develop an understanding of this. That a product produced without their disciplines could have an enviable reputation was not something which few incomers even bothered to understand. Thus at that time a Leyland drawing would attract the reputation of being a form of minor deity to be obeyed without query. Shop floor experience, therefore, could not bail the coach works out of the abyss into which it was falling. Although there is no strong evidence to say that this long stop had ever been used, its very efficacy would banish the evidence without ever seeing the light of day.

There was tremendous pressure from NBC to deliver the vehicles and therefore no prototype was built on a Leopard chassis – the RE update produced earlier was no more than a styling exercise (a 'wangle' in coachworks parlance) as the structure was left completely untouched. Further, those were the dying days of centralised engineering and any change to the drawings and specifications handed down was not to be permitted. In any event no one was ever very willing to come down from Leyland to take an interest in features which were their concern.

Worse was to come during assembly. The recollection of many of the coachbuilders involved are very clear to this day. They recall that it was necessary to build the bodies in a banana shape, pointing upwards, if there was to be any chance of the emergency and boot doors closing when the body inevitably settled immediately after build! A stark contrast to the days of Alf Tattersall, who when he was general manager could be expected to take his jacket off and set to work on the shop floor to resolve problems. Even as the first vehicle went on its maiden voyage the flexing of the rear of the body was so great as to be visible.

Sadly the fears of ECW people were very quickly realised, and after scarcely one week's service the news came from United Counties that the boot had fallen out of one of its vehicles used on the short express services from Northampton and Luton to Victoria. Severe cracking was found elsewhere in the rear structure. Remedial design work obviously had to be considered and vehicles were withdrawn for modification.

The problems did not stop there, and the flexing of the thin windscreen canopy led to the new style (heavy) windscreens parting company with their bodies as they went along the road! Almost concurrently cracks appeared in the rear dome and substructure. The shorter PSU3 Leopard variant had the larger full bay rear emergency door to a new Leyland design intended to cure the long term problems experienced on the 1972 RE coach bodies. Unfortunately the complexity and weight of the replacement was such that its weight caused hinges and lightweight frames to bend, doors to sag and refuse to close.

Although ECW, on behalf of Leyland, responded to the inevitable cries from its undoubtedly most important single customer, the shortest lives of B51 bodies were some of those with National Travel West. These had been built to a higher interior specification on 12-metre Tiger 245 chassis frames. Full soft trim was specified, as was a coach entrance door. Some of the bodies were scrapped after a mere two years, others following after slightly longer periods, when even their owners gave up the struggle as opportunity presented itself. The few remaining have received much rework, but the poor quality of so much of the body means that this class is the one which will have the shortest lives ever for modern day production from the coach works.

The cost was great. During the build and warranty periods the profitability of the plant suffered as the costs were directly charged. As so many vehicles were involved, teams had to be sent out to operators premises, quite apart from those vehicles returned to Lowestoft. It is believed that NBC pressure was such that some were sent to outside concerns such as Wadham Stringer. Even beyond the financial damage, a promising line of diversification, so soon to be needed as privatisation loomed, was firmly severed. The image of the plant was tarnished beyond quick recall, especially as all was not well with the new Olympian body for National Bus.

Olympic Heights?

The Olympian was conceived at Leyland upon a Marcus Smith initiative and appropriately all the prototype chassis development was carried out at Bristol on the floor of the experimental shop led by Len Norman and Don Templar, respectively experimental shop manager and resident engineer. The astute will notice that the plant level senior engineer had been demeaned to this status.

In preparing the body, Leyland Bus personnel had taken much of the Titan shell and altered it to meet the 13ft 8in overall height objective to suit NBC. The approach was obviously justified and the savings implicit in the commonality of side glasses upstairs and down, as well as upstairs on the Titan, was useful. Similarly the thought that ECW and Charles Roe should follow a common approach to bodying the new chassis was commendable. It did not happen quite like that, and both builders adapted build to their own ways. Any attempt to follow central dictate would have stopped deliveries long before they had even commenced. Notwithstanding this individuality nearly 40 years of evolution and proven structural integrity were thrown away. Out went the continuous rails which gave the structure its safe passenger compartment, out went tried extrusions, panelling and trimming methods. What long term benefits came in is more difficult to quantify.

One thing which did of course happen was that working drawings from Leyland were initially followed as were material specifications. The old problems of lower-deck floor structures and leaking panels returned with a vengeance. They were cured after pressure from the plant and users, but the coach works reputation simply did not need this further blow. Coach works personnel certainly refer to the inevitability of these problems, simply as a result of the lack experience and unwillingness to listen of those who purported to design the new bodies compared with the steady evolution which had occurred from 1944 to 1981.

Local Ability ?

Towards the end, the tendency towards central engineering had gone – as indeed had Park Royal Vehicles and Charles Roe, leaving ECW as the only Leyland Bus traditional body builder. Strenuous efforts were put into special versions of the Olympian, as described elsewhere in this book. There was a genuine willingness to believe that there was a future for the plant. As time went on, functional requirements alone were supplied to the coach works on general arrangement (GA) drawings for the host of export variants. Coach factory personnel then used their unwritten experience and skills to produce vehicles to meet the need of the customer. In many ways this would be frowned upon in the 'nineties, as certain of the disciplines Leyland had tried to impose without thought in the 'seventies are now enshrined in Quality Standard BS5750. This is the goal of much of manufacturing industry, yet undoubtedly ECW delivered the goods over so many years with its own form of discipline and customer support.

Many former coach works personnel refer to the spirit of the plant which triumphed to deliver one-off prototype vehicles, on time, and to specification within the constraints of unsatisfactory initial engineering. This is the spirit of Tattersall and his predecessors triumphing once more. The use of craftsmen obviates the need for strictly production

An Olympian, destined to be East Midland 327 (C 327 HWJ), is seen outside the factory ready for delivery if not service. By this time ECW was out-shopping a proportion of vehicles to be finished by the customer's own paint shop.

engineered drawings – if the unskilled are to use them rather like an 'Airfix' kit, each process needs to be both laboriously spelled out – and slavishly followed. This approach does become essential for mass-production using unskilled assembly labour, of course.

Sameness

The operator looks for commonality as well as value for money when seeking to renew his fleet. But life is not that simple, and the United Kingdom bus industry has long been a political football – sometimes for good, sometimes for evil. Over the recent life of the Coach Works one major bloc of operators was tied to Lowestoft for its vehicles, followed by the extension of this tie to another fiercely independent group. Did they lose out thus?

Apart from the commonality of construction methods, ECW used to carry over many body fittings between designs. Additionally, where possible there was a tendency to use the same basic parts on succeeding designs. Thus the

This didn't often happen but in 1983 ECW was still able to construct two further VRT bodies for NBC on existing VRT frames. One of the two, East Kent 7655 (XJJ 655V) stands hopefully in the Lowestoft yard awaiting a second chance to be of better service to its owner.

FLF Lodekka and the first VRTs share upper-deck front windows, side windows and rearmost upper-deck bays. The examples are legion but a pattern is emerging.

ECW had a policy of developing its own suppliers such that 'the company', but more importantly the suppliers' operatives knew the needs of 'the coach works', and the personnel on the shop floor thus busied themselves with an objective, long bred into them. 'Once a supplier, always a supplier' is too strong an assertion, but coachworks personnel do not speak of many changes over the years. Good quality suppliers' products are generally to be trusted – choice based on price alone will, if the specification is not tight enough, lead to trouble in the end.

The Tilling Group, both via the British Transport Commission and subsequently the Transport Holding Company used to 'play' the commodities markets to the advantage of both their coach works and operators. Thus they bought aluminium, copper and wood forward and, at times, the stores at Lowestoft would be more than full. Yet this did not necessarily matter, the price and the quality were both right. This policy came to an end in the late 'sixties and into the 'seventies, partly because the National Bus Company did not retain the headquarters control over plant activities but more importantly because the Leyland share deals transferred day-to-day responsibility to Leyland itself. The, perhaps, unique arrangements came to an end and although plant level buying continued for a while, the

Leyland Bus group established a divisional purchasing group based at the AEC plant at Southall in the days when a so-called Headquarters functioned from there. Since this occurred in the late 'seventies, relatively little attention was paid to the principal Lowestoft product, the VRT body, apart from trying to incorporate sundry Leyland National body fittings to the vehicle. Many would say the reverse would have made more sense.

B45 Olympian and new Suppliers

The Olympian was seen as a 'Group' product, and therefore experienced purchasing personnel at both Bristol and Lowestoft were cyphers to enact group decisions on sourcing. It would be wrong to assert that group decisions were inherently wrong simply by their origin. BUT, and that corruption of the syntax of the English language is a big one, in establishing any new supplier there is a learning curve to be followed and several such were involved, all of which impinged upon the customer. Two such came to the fore recently in discussion with former coachworks personnel. These matters, apparently really only of plant level significance, only become relevant when the vital effect on customer and reputation within a new supply framework is considered.

Traditionally the batch system ensured that sufficient components were in production – or on order – to be available when required for assembly. The company's pulse was dependent on this system – so was the all important bonus ! The new regime jeopardised this. Not only were suppliers different – and unaccustomed to the ways of the plant – but a strict regime ordered only sufficient material for exactly the number of bodies required to be built. This had two effects. Firstly if anyone made a mistake, however simple and understandable, and there was the inevitable shortfall, the last vehicles in the batch could not be completed. This appears to have happened on numerous occasions. Secondly if the batch of raw material was rejected, *en bloc*, mayhem resulted !

The problems occasioned by this change of culture in the material supply sphere have been debated amongst production managers, finance controllers and supplies personnel for years. However the practical effects for the coach works are recounted by former chief inspector George Crisp, supported by his quality control manager Sam Catts. In the first instance a new supplier of aluminium extrusions from Scotland replaced ECW's two traditional sources. At risk was a batch of 56 Olympians. In the face of total intransigence ECW's quality control team was obliged to reject whole consignments of aluminium sections, not once but two or three times. Material stocks were then so low that body construction could not begin, with all that that implied.

The reason for rejection was quite clear. The aluminium extrusions had to exhibit various specific hardness characteristics as they were required to be formed into various components – some of which provided a crucial part of the body strength. If the material was incorrect, the body might simply shatter in an impact collision. The need to merge cost effectiveness, minimisation of stocks and yet timely delivery to the customer is difficult to achieve, yet ECW achieved it satisfactorily for decades before Leyland became involved.

The Ministry

The second instance only further serves to emphasise the different environment, and the conflict between a car manufacturing philosophy determined to save even half a penny, and a considered view of the long term. Again the Olympian was involved and on this occasion fifteen coaches were involved. These vehicles were 'Specials' for which many parts were designed and sourced locally.

The glass in a PSV in the UK is quite rigidly specified and it must be of safety or laminated pattern marked to certify compliance with British Standard. The particular batch arrived, was not certified, and was rejected. The supplier attended the coach works and marked it up locally with a mark correct to its type, but not appropriate to the application. The Chief Inspector again recorded a rejection.

Now in any manufacturing plant a procedure exists whereby in the absence of the correct materials a 'Deviation' can be raised to permit use of the nearest acceptable substitute. This was imposed at the behest of the commercial department, not as in days gone by in the engineering area. However in the bus world matters are not that simple and each vehicle has to be certified as fit for public service (involving the grant of a Certificate of Initial Fitness at that time) by an Area Mechanical Engineer of the Department of Transport. This official came, saw, and rejected the fifteen coaches. Thus Leyland could not deliver and reputedly had to pay penalties for its late performance, in addition to the delays and lost bonus on the shop floor.

A strange culture

Why is it necessary to relate these issues? Quite simply to emphasise the change in culture between 1965 and 1987 and more importantly its knock-on effect on customer relations and industrial relations in the factory.

New management will always bring new methods. The culture of the management is explored elsewhere in this book but the customer grows accustomed to, and gains confidence from, a certain philosophy on the part of his supplier. Change to one can be at the peril of the other as has ultimately been the case.

Outside interference in even small matters from those who do not fully understand the results of their actions can be very damaging in any situation where routines and labour are totally inter-dependent. When the perpetrators are short-term career orientated, and can leave someone else with the problem, the results can be catastrophic. Fifty years ago someone might have considered that rarely had so many been put out of work by so few so easily.

The Coach Works is still missed. Its products will be its lasting epitaph for many years to come in tribute to the shameless waste of another industrial asset.

Twelve of Men, Management and Politics

For the first forty years of its life, ECW attracted a succession of Yorkshiremen to its management – Bill Bramham, Ralph Sugden, Ronnie Statham and finally Alf Tattersall. There was nothing particularly curious in that but they did bring with them the Yorkshireman's parsimony.

In some ways this was a blessing as the coachworks was able to continue to develop as a compliant in-house supplier, yet one which also supplied a quality product with good profits and a (then) commendably small appetite for capital investment to secure these praiseworthy attributes. An old fashioned approach, not one to be decried, but at odds with the world of car manufacturing into which a Labour Government, by a sequence of events some seemingly quite opposite in intent, was to plunge the plant and which ultimately led to its demise.

The British bus industry has long featured in the aspirations of politicians as a means of furthering the political aims that each espouses. ECW, with its relationship with operating companies – United Automobile, Eastern Counties and then the Tilling Group – was sucked into this maelstrom and in 1947 was nationalised for its trouble. There was much controversy and opposition to the nationalisation which not only encompassed certain bus operators and the railways, but also brought in much of the road haulage industry.

Whether politics was a less doctrinaire or more gentlemanly activity in those days is worthy of a book in itself, but for whatever reason the Labour Government of the day accepted a (Conservative) amendment in the House of Commons which effectively prevented ECW and its chassis manufacturing associate, Bristol Tramways and Carriage Company Ltd from selling to those undertakings not in the direct ownership of the British Transport Commission. A curiosity in this regard has to be Walter Alexander, the Scottish Coachbuilder (then of Stirling), which enjoyed a similar status in relation to the Alexander bus operating company yet which was not included in the nationalisation plans. Another example of the canniness of the Scot, perhaps ?

Whatever the machinations of the day, ECW duly passed into public ownership in 1948. There then followed a period of eighteen years when ECW continued with the

Earlier in this book we showed management with the 1000th Lodekka, Here is another view taken the same day, this time with the coach builders.

business of building bus bodies (not forgetting a few cabs for Bristol's thriving truck business). Bus bodies which were often admired, if not for their innovative styling, certainly for their quality. These were, however, the days of the gentlemen whose stewardship saw the remission of very substantial profits back to the headquarters of BTC – especially if nothing went into capital investment at the coachworks!

Although road haulage and the steel manufacturing industry, amongst others, were returned to the private sector, road passenger transport and bus manufacturing was left in the public sector, possibly because the former owners did not want it back! Certainly 'Denationalisation' (the then term for what we currently call 'Privatisation') seemed to consist of returning the assets to their former owners rather than the approach currently adopted.

It was therefore in 1965 that Anthony Wedgewood Benn, a member of Harold Wilson's second administration, and MP for the constituency in which the Bristol works was located, hit upon the idea of the share exchange with two Leyland subsidiaries – Park Royal Vehicles Limited and Charles H. Roe Limited – to release Bristol and ECW from the sales bondage they had endured in the preceding fifteen years. At this stage it was limited to a minority holding in ECW and Bristol Commercial Vehicles, so control was still in THC hands.

Throughout this time ECW had been managed by a dedicated band of men who had a full knowledge of the various aspects of their job – and the confidence of their parent company directors such that they were allowed to get on with the job. The company was managed from 1948 through to the early 'seventies by a Board comprised of the General Manager and various headquarters representatives of the Tilling Group. The list of Directors and Chairmen reads as it were the list of the great and the good of the industry. Board meetings usually took place at monthly intervals although the Directors were frequent visitors to the plant.

Despair Ahoy !

The rot set in, however, around 1970 when Leyland increased its shareholding to fifty percent – held via Bus Manufacturers Holdings Limited. Although the National Bus Company was nominally an equal partner, the crucial point was that management control was conceded to British Leyland. T. W. H. (Tony) Gailey was the last busman to be Chairman and he handed the position over to Ronald Ellis of Leyland Motors in September 1969. Ellis was a fighter, and headed up the variously named truck operations as well as ECW. His determination to see fair play and investment for the commercial vehicles, as opposed to the unbelievable regime creating vast losses on the car side, may well have ruffled feathers in high places. Whatever the truth of the matter he was removed, at extremely short notice, and promoted sideways to the position of the Government's chief arms salesman. Whilst, inevitably perhaps, he was not universally popular, he is remembered as the last busman Leyland had at its helm. As one replacement followed another Leyland subsequently plumbed the depths of despair and ineptitude, and so too did ECW's fortunes wane.

Experimentation continued in the 'sixties: this FLF for Eastern Counties has fixed upper deck windows. Ventilation was provided by the five bi-directional Vortex Ventilators on the roof. The experiment was not judged a success.

A new version of the FLF was introduced even as the last orders were being completed. The vehicles for Eastern National were a complete anachronism in being the only English examples to the longer length – yet only having the same number of seats as the normal vehicle! These vehicles also managed to avoid being swopped with SBG later in the great exchange of VRTs for Lodekkas.

In 1968 the British Leyland Motor Corporation was created out of a notional merger between British Motor Holdings and the Leyland Motor Corporation. BMH was days from receivership when Harold Wilson persuaded Sir Donald Stokes that the successful Leyland Motor Corporation should be pleased to takeover the carmaker. Stokes was ennobled for his trouble whilst the new Leyland Group found the pound in its pocket was not so much devalued as vaporised. Leyland all but went to the wall – and was supported lavishly by the state over many years ! That decision began a long period where funds were diverted from commercial vehicles to cars and a new breed of manager came in.

Group 'Managers'

These were the personnel department's professionals, and the 'number crunchers' whose abacuses were temperamental at best and produced flawed policies at worst. As the 'seventies unfolded their influence grew and whilst existing personnel at various manufacturing plants saw their status and reward diminished, their successors often took pride in not being versed in the activities of the plants they purported to manage. Strangely, their longevity in post was not noteworthy.

In many traditionally managed plants such as ECW, accession to the top office frequently brought with it a

Rover or Triumph motor car – then the height of achievement, with side benefits. As early as 1970 British Leyland was trying to force its standard terms on people and as a financially challenged enterprise that often meant that the heads of successful businesses were brought down either to the level of the lowest or more particularly down to a lower level simply because their plant was smaller than that of someone else.

Reward by size of plant was virtually linked to size of losses so far as the car plants were concerned but the brave and blinkered battled on with their policies and created the situation where British Leyland's motor cars and workforce became a national joke. Disenchantment and the urge to leave if at all possible became prevalent at higher levels.

New Faces and New Ways

The average age of influential Leyland personnel began to fall, and many appointments were made from amongst the ranks of personnel trained by other car manufacturers, notably Ford. Frequently their ways were American in origin. This cannot be condemned in itself when applied to the mass production of Cortinas when parts were costed down to several decimal places but when Colchester Corporation wanted to modify some features for an order for half a dozen buses, it was quite crudely plain stupid.

In any event, even in the car plants, the task was only half done. The ingredient which was missing was that a management philosophy cannot be moved as if it were a rose bush. Wait until October, water and hope! Or maybe that was the problem. The philosophy of management in Ford was an entity in itself and the culture was both entrenched and well developed. The psychological testing

As the first share exchanges were taking place ECW was planning the range of buses which it intended to take it into the next era. The ideas were to be shown at the 1966 Commercial Motor Show.

The cab of one exhibit, an RE for United Auto, is seen here on the ECW stand. Clearly there is either some untypical muddled thinking or else this exhibition vehicle was intended to show various options. United R66 had two doors, then coming into favour for one-man-operation and also semi-automatic transmission. These features can be seen in the cab switch gear. The glass partitioning to the rear of the driver would have given a much needed feel of spaciousness (although it was to be troublesome later) – yet the pole and partition to the cab side would make fare collection from the cab nigh impossible.

A scene from Eastern Way also in the summer of 1966 shows two of the other show exhibits being fitted out. In the left door can be seen the two VRX prototypes with GGM on the left. Just peeking out of the far door is one of Crosville's three dual-purpose RELL6G vehicles, one of which is preserved by Northern Bus.

of potential managers became more important than their records. In Leyland it was an anathema to many who had been doing their jobs successfully for years and simply saw no reason to change because a couple of car plants were continually on strike, or else the butt of every latter day music hall joke imaginable.

There were many who thought Morecambe and Wise would have run rings round Leyland's so-called whizz kids – the joke about car workers signing the visitor's book instead of clocking in perhaps said it all.

Against this background, many very capable men were relieved to be able to take retirement from the maelstrom, Alf Tattersall included.

Enter John Bloor

Alf Tattersall was succeeded by John Bloor. Bloor's appointment was clearly a Leyland one, but ECW was very fortunate to gain a man who had substantial experience in PSV as well as car body building, the last time that the former qualification was deemed necessary for anyone holding the post. Bloor's early career had seen him move from Austin Morris to Rover (where he was involved in the earliest stages of the design of the Range Rover) and subsequently to Guy Motors in the wake of its takeover by Jaguar. A move to MCW in 1967 took him into PSV body engineering and subsequently he became Chief Body Engineer at Park Royal Vehicles. Ironically he was to report to PRV's plant Director Bill Shirley, who had moved across from the equivalent post at Lowestoft in 1953. John Bloor was at least a man who was more used to the new rough and tumble of management within the Leyland Group.

Changing Times

There had also been a shift in the importance of the finance function (often now having a disproportionate role in decision making at plant level) and each plant now had a finance controller. This was in part to enable remote and notionally independent profit centres – for that was now the status of once-proud companies in the Leyland empire – to apply group disciplines to ensure that as much money was retained at the centre as was unrealistically possible. The incumbent at Lowestoft in John Bloor's early years was Geoff Medler.

Throughout the Bloor years there were changes on two key fronts. Firstly the management turmoil and political in-fighting at Leyland level, and secondly the need to make changes at ECW such that his masters could not fault the coach works' performance.

All was not bleak, as Bloor clearly seemed to understand the needs of ECW. Production was still on an echelon principle with teams of three working on various aspects of build – often with inadequate equipment such as scaffolds, and trestles. Decades of chronic non-investment still meant that the intermediate roofs of double-deckers were, quite literally, thrown into place by calling upon the service of workers who happened to be nearby, and that roofs proper were carried the length of the shop by a group, rather like pall bearers, on 12ft-long poles and thus offered

to the part assembled bodies!!

Sid Wright gave unhesitating confirmation that the purse strings were certainly released under Bloor and Medler. Not only were funds found to address handling (notwithstanding possible action by the Health and Safety Executive) but the company's housing stock was improved and even increased. This was, of course another aspect of employment at the coach works. As people progressed through the ranks they aspired firstly to a company house and subsequently to a better company house. It was always said that in Lowestoft a visitor could identify a coach works house – either it was painted in Tilling colours or, if the doorbell was rung twice, it moved off!

The bonus scheme had long been a key part of the wage structure at Lowestoft. Each shop negotiated its own deal led by its shop steward. This meant that bonuses did not necessarily reflect saleable complete buses, and much depended on the sharpness of the individual shop steward. A further problem in times of fast approaching change (the Olympian body built in a manner completely at odds with ECW's traditional methods was looming) was that a 'price' had to be fixed for each new process before adoption was really underway, thus leading to potential over-generous payments through inexperience. This was at least partially replaced by a finished bus scheme based on a certain amount for each double-decker, 0.6 of that for a single-decker, and various special amounts for complex one-off or high value vehicles.

John Bloor recalls that one of the first tasks he faced was to raise the morale at the coach works and to give people the will to succeed. He tackled this in two ways. He recognised that he was the stranger, the first incomer at a senior level for many years. He gathered both the senior managers and the shop stewards (led by Ben Pitcher) together to get his message of future prosperity across. Realising that it was not getting back to the shop floor as he wanted, he took the message out himself, holding meetings in each shop, using any convenient bench as his soapbox. The approach paid dividends, for he is always remembered for being approachable by the men. The aloofness of his predecessors had gone – partly due to the generation change.

Many people visiting the plant at the time commented upon it giving the impression of being an anachronism from the Victorian age, yet it was successful and extremely profitable. After closure one Leyland contract manager with many years bodybuilding experience under his belt confessed he didn't know how they did it! Maybe that was always Leyland's problem – they didn't know either.

One of the earliest things Bloor introduced was line building and the De Mag cranes to move those intermediate roofs about. Similarly the factory roof was repaired: years of rain pouring into the body shop were brought to an end. Other major reorganisations saw stores turned into production areas and vice versa, though parts required for immediate build were now stored at the lineside to ease construction. The famous wooden doors fronting Eastern Way were even replaced by lightweight aluminium ones (what else?!) by 1981.

Another farewell around this time was said to the traditional 30ft bus body. These two views show a dual-purpose variant, Bristol MW5G DFE 166D, for Lincolnshire. Notice how the traditional inlaid leather work is still to be found on the seat backs. The whole vehicle has that indefinable air of being 'right' – an ECW trademark for decades.

Sickness and Safety

The one benefit immediately felt by the shop floor workers after Leyland took control was the emergence of a sick pay scheme and pension plan similar to that enjoyed at all other Leyland plants. By now shop stewards were beginning to travel to other plants as the coach work's representatives on some of these pan-Leyland Schemes. The experience was not wasted. Lowestoft, quite unbelievably for a plant of its size, could now boast its first ever medical centre with qualified staff rather than a well meaning first aider. A comment dropped casually into a conversation was that most members of the saw mill gang could demonstrate the loss of at least one finger during their careers, so the improved facility would probably be useful.

It would be wrong to say that up to the 'seventies ECW had ignored its duties to provide for employees safety. However the onset of the then new safety legislation led to a number of investments of which the De Mag crane was but one. Others, not as well received, were the virtual total replacement of three phase electric hand tools by De Souter air driven equipment. They were not as well received for the electric tools were faster and more powerful, (important to the bonus scheme) as well as a great deal easier to use.

Ryder

Throughout his years in office John Bloor was confronted with the task not met by his predecessors. He was now trying to run a business which few of his directors understood, and probably fewer cared about. The focus of attention was always on the car divisions. The Ryder Report, written by Sir Don Ryder, (later to be Baron Ryder) promised devolution of decision making back to the lowest level. This was taken by the misguided or the trusting to mean plant level. Unfortunately those pious sentiments were worthless. The divisional directors were having none of that and demoralised plant management came to believe even Plant Directors were seen as being inferior to staff employed at divisional level.

Things at Leyland went from bad to worse. Doug Jack's chronicle of the fall of the Leyland Bus empire tells the story from the inside. In 1979/80, Desmond Pitcher who had notionally been a director of the coach works from 1976/8 was sacked as Managing Director of Leyland Vehicles Ltd and was replaced by David Abel. He was a straight numbers man, and, ominously, Marcus Smith, who had been a busman, in charge of the bus business was an early casualty. He was replaced by another accountant William Kenneth McIver as Managing Director in 1979. He had little feeling for the bus business, those above him less. Despite its original engineering prowess having led the world's bus industry both Leyland and Government now treated the bus business merely as a sideline. This did not bode well for a highly skilled plant, miles from anywhere on Leyland's imperial map.
The late 'seventies saw a period of consistent output with a full order book. Indeed in 1977/78 National Bus was forced to give Willowbrook an order for 57 bodies on Bristol VRT/SL chassis simply because ECW could not cope with them having 550 such bodies in its 1978 programme. These were not the most successful bodies ever, but the lesson was not learned and worse was to come from Loughborough – and yet that in itself was to herald the B51 body...

The Titan cometh ...

Leyland's Truck and Bus Division had rightly been looking to the future and there were designs for replacing the Leyland Atlantean, now in its AN68 form, the Daimler Fleetline (albeit now produced in less satisfactory form at Leyland headquarters) and indeed the Bristol VRT, beloved of the National Bus Company. All three would fail to meet forthcoming European legislation and the product that was intended to take Leyland into the future was the B15, subsequently badged as 'Titan'. The design work was undertaken in Lancashire and Park Royal Vehicles built the prototypes. Assembly duly started at Park Royal which had considerable experience in the task through being the major assembler of the Routemaster. Unfortunately union demands related to the proposed recruitment of semi-skilled labour caused tremendous internal problems and production virtually stopped. At the same time there were ideas in Leyland headquarters about moving the assembly line to the old AEC site, but before anything could be discussed at PRV the controlling Labour members of the Greater London Council trumpeted this plan – to their ultimate embarrassment.

The idea did not work out and a combination of the high demand for skilled labour in north London and abysmal industrial relations not helped by long distance management from Leyland, led to a need to find the product a new home. A comparison here between the car mentality of Leyland group management and proven bus building practice was beginning to emerge. Traditionally a bus would be designed around the strengths, weaknesses and experience of its manufacturer. In the late 'seventies British Leyland's car building subsidiaries had toted various models about the country in search of stable industrial relations – Triumph Dolomite and TR7 upped and moved to and from Speke on Merseyside to Coventry and the Rover SD1 saloon was evicted from its purpose-built plant at Solihull, which was ultimately to be the new home of Land Rover, to Morris' volume plant at Cowley in Oxford. Hindsight has judged the quality – poorly – of British Leyland cars of the period. Yet buses were to be subject to the same strategy and not for the last time as consideration of viability of Leyland Bus' plants, including the coach works demonstrates.

The Titan, having been dispossessed at either of its intended London homes, was offered to the coach works. There now follows one of the saddest and possibly misguided disputes in a land which had become throughout Europe for apparently senseless industrial confrontation.

The possibility of the Titan coming to Lowestoft was first aired publicly in the Eastern Daily Press of 12th September, 1979. At the time it was firmly denied on the

The final farewell was to the SU body which had been derived from the MW. Western National EDV 551D has its face to the wall but reveals that the SU body had the same rear screen as the SC4LK bodies.

basis that the coach factory had a full order book stretching two years ahead. However by the end of that November firm plans were being talked of for a £2.5 million investment which would add 300 new jobs to the existing 980. Progress was rapid and, by the Christmas break, test bores had been carried out and an application for planning consent had been lodged with Waveney District Council. The plan was to construct a new 90,000sq ft factory on the Eastern Way site (on the sports fields) for the complete assembly of the vehicle. Although various concerns were raised, outline planning consent was readily given. This was not without its hiccoughs but after the sort of negotiation normal in such matters, full consent was forthcoming. The prospects of new employment saw to that. That was the easy part.

.....and goeth again

Obviously an agreement was needed with the work force, as many of the operations involved were new to the coach works, although there was experience of working on integral vehicles over the years – the Bristol LS and Lodekkas are properly thus regarded – upon the definition of a self supporting frame. Slightly earlier, the coach works – with some assistance from Bristol whose General Manager was then still A J Romer – had designed the chassis and mechanical aspects of the Dennis-based integrals of 1949. The initial proposition was therefore that ECW would build bodies on Titan frames brought from Workington. Strangely, not wholly assembled at ECW as at Park Royal. Doug Jack's *Beyond Reality – Leyland Bus, The Twilight Years.*(Venture Publications) refers to the apparently secret assembly of a Titan

underframe with (temporary) bracing at Farington, for assessment of the task. It is known that LTE Titan T160 (CUL160 V) spent some time at ECW but there are some recollections, by influential personnel at Lowestoft, that the underframe was also presented at the coach works (presumably prior to its going to Cumbria) as part of the process of 'selling what amounted to a contract to build the vehicle there'. A curiously strange way for Head Office to treat its manufacturing units but an apparent form of competition prevalent in the car sector which was to cost ECW dear.

Serious negotiations started in January 1980 and although Leyland itself, to this day, maintains its traditional insistence upon skilled/time served labour working in its now one remaining truck assembly plant, the influence of the car divisions and the comparative success of production at Workington dictated that Leyland would be making great play about 'unskilled people being recruited to assemble a new bus'. London Transport itself was known to prefer transfer to Lowestoft (scarcely a surprise when it is realised that Marcus Smith, late of BCV and the National Bus Company and the Leyland Bus Division was Managing Director). The inescapable logic was that Titan was still a coachbuilt vehicle for which such skills were important. The day of the main negotiation dawned and the Union delegation was led by Mr McGowan of the Transport and General Workers Union. He was the senior East Anglian official but, strangely, he was accompanied

Whilst life was inexorably changing with the ranks of the management, outwardly only the vehicle liveries changed a little and the fruits of the Leyland deal were not seen for the poisoned objects they were ultimately to prove. Here we see that ECW was still producing versions of its bus body for Lincolnshire Road Car to use on its long distance services to London. It is to be hoped that additional sound deadening material was used on KVL 454 H always assuming its Perkins engine was powerful enough to propel it.

ECW also made its third appearance at the Commercial Motor Show, having its own stand at Earls Court. One of the exhibits was this LH6P for Eastern Counties. HAH 537 L.

by equally senior officials from Leyland headquarters who had never previously had any connection with the Lowestoft plant and its industrial relations.

The Leyland personnel made no secret of the fact that they saw the task as better belonging to them and to Workington. The recollections of local shop stewards are quite clear on the point that a package was laid 'on the table' which would have brought new people into the coach works and who would very quickly have been paid the full local rate for the same jobs also done in the 'old' plant. There are two crucial points here. Quite apart from the aspect of the low pay years of the traditional apprenticeship served by everyone at the coachworks, tools were to be supplied by the company. This was quite new, for each coach work's craftsman provided his own tools, at his own expense. These tools did not come cheap and it is here that part of the origin of the much vaunted – yet incorrect – tale of a demand for £5,000 per man compensation emanates.

The second element of the package is that no account was apparently taken about the one thing around which the Lowestoft wage structure was built – the bonus. Traditionally shop-based, this was keenly fought over by both shop stewards and plant management. The term semi-skilled was freely used by Leyland Bus industrial relations specialists in a plant which took pride in its craft. No place was left for their dignity or contribution to something in which local people were acutely aware the future might lie. Yet no one disagreed that the new workers could not be apprentice trained – sufficient did not exist. The local shop stewards are adamant to this day that their own full time local and national officials overtly prevented both discussion or negotiation and insisted that a crude unrefined deal was put to a vote of the 500 craftsmen (only) without further ado. There was never any doubt which way such a vote would go – to attack so many of the basic tenets of the coachbuilders pride and hard fought dignity in one go, inevitably courted decisive rejection. That this happened on 24th January was neither surprise nor disappointment to those who had travelled to Lowestoft to lead the negotiations. To some it is, perhaps, strange that a trades union would avoid negotiating a local deal knowing that a group of its members would reject it otherwise.

There was then a further period of negotiations and reassurance on individuals terms and status and not a little conjecture over the alleged £5,000 demand by the craftsmen. Efforts were made on the following Tuesday to cajole the men into further discussions but there was little of substance in the message. On the morning of the 5th February the talks started but did not progress. They finally broke down that evening. Curiously the company was the only party to comment extensively to the press, speaking of assurances about skills and apparently offering to 'top up' the bonus pool during the training period. Eric Bone of the National Union did break his peace saying that problem was over some form of remuneration and poured scorn both on the issue of the £5,000 and the offer on the bonus pool. He spoke of £1,000 and £10 per week per man. The lack of substantial reaction by the trades union was to remain, despite heavy press criticism of the workforce, even the national press commenting upon this stance.

The day after, the whole of the plant shop stewards committee resigned – and not, surviving members say, at the action of the workforce, rather "the feeling of betrayal they felt on the part of their own national brothers".

The Truth

The truth lies in the answer to the simple question who is my member? The trade union nationally saw Workington's need as by far the greater. There had already been a marked swing to double-deckers yet the market for single-deckers was virtually non-existent. Indeed in 1982 a mere 71 Leyland Nationals were built, falling away to 64 in 1983 and 33 in 1985 in a factory designed to build 40 such vehicles per week! Workington in 1980 was seen as having no future and therefore it was not unnatural that certain people were prepared to adopt a strategy to resolve this – one way or another. Titan was seen as a way of spreading work about the Leyland Bus plants, the thought being that ECW's traditional NBC market together with a share of the other sectors would keep both going. Even before the talks at Eastern Way were convened the unions and plant level management at Workington had reached a no-cost-deal to build a conventional bus, probably a piece of opportunism by plant management. The union having achieved what it considered an agreement in the interests of its membership at large no longer had any need of the Lowestoft arrangement. On the other side, plants bidding against one another for the lowest cost means of building individual products was now an acceptable way of life for certain plant managers and therefore McIver and Leyland Bus had secured its financial objective. Neither had any material interest in a positive vote from the coach works, probably quite the opposite. At the time of the abortive negotiations the national official of the Union summed the position up when he warned local officials by saying this (Titan) is a road down which you must not go, and after the coach works finally closed in 1987 the local area official admitted to George Crisp, one of the shop stewards gagged in 1981, that it is the union's job to look after all its members – and that it must be remembered includes those in equally remote Cumbria where the TGWU dominated.

Reaction

Inevitably the press and industry reacted quite strongly to what was presented by the Leyland Press Office as a snub to those proffering a secure future. Many appeals were made to the two sides, led by Jim Prior, who was both the local member of Parliament and a leading member of the Government. This time Leyland was the one to claim hurt dignity whilst the coachbuilders were left leaderless and seemingly whingeing at something which could not or would not be understood by laymen – their craft. The reaction was predictable condemnation of the workforce – and to some degree the company for only allowing a couple of weeks for the talks. Ominously McIver issued a statement to the press saying that the short term future was safe,

Sales to non NBC operators were not under the control of Leyland and many successes were achieved. This is the rear view of Ipswich Atlantean PDRI LDX 73F, of 1968.

although there were economies of bodying the Titan and Olympian together if such a site were to become available. However after about five years there would be an element of doubt.

Workington's offer

Many will ask why Leyland people, having spent so much on planning the new factory and pushing to trial bores and planning consent, simply packed their bags and scuttled back to Preston. The answer may partly lie in the fact that they had an alternative bid from the Workington plant management for Titan and the trade union had quietly offered to deliver an agreement on manning in return for the investment. Workington's bid was apparently cheaper and if nothing else a labour agreement would be forthcoming without the loss of face implicit in going back to Lowestoft. Their thoughts were already conditioned by the open hostility of Margaret Thatcher (see again *Beyond Reality*) and their distant hopes that they might be able to stage a management buyout of parts of the business. The willingness to contract and indeed to sacrifice the traditional plants to support Workington's future was now gaining momentum.

To Ken McIver, then Leyland Bus' soon-to-be-ousted Managing Director, are the final words " ...you will simply wither on the vine". What was not said was that help was to be forthcoming to achieve this end.

The 'Eighties

Having repelled the Titan, ECW was now in a position where it could have pulled through, but a position nonetheless which was potentially vulnerable. The demand for buses was dropping away gradually. In its constant search for reductions in public spending the Government quite quickly removed new bus grant between April 1980 and March 1984. This grant payable on compliant new buses had started in 1968, reaching 50% of the purchase price under Ted Heath's administration. The grant had achieved its objective of allowing British bus operators to renew their outdated fleets and at the same time to make provision for one-man-operation. News of the Grant's demise (started by the Labour Government but accelerated by Margaret Thatcher) hastened orders which were in the pipeline to create an artificial market. Subsequently, orders were scaled down such that the Charles Roe plant was sacrificed in 1984, indeed six part-built vehicles intended for Yorkshire Rider were even transferred to Lowestoft for completion. Two cornerstones of Margaret Thatcher's policies were to prove the demise of ECW – together with

Another promising line was the ongoing sales of REs throughout the country. The South Wales municipalities were steady customers and Gelligaer KTX 243 L was particularly attractive. In 1975 Leyland Headquarters sent an order that the RE moulds and jigs were to be destroyed to remove the plant's ability to compete with that Cumbrian cuckoo, the Leyland National.

But not everything changed: Lincolnshire was there again for bus-derived vehicles for its express services throughout 1970-2, by then favouring the dual-purpose bodied RELH. This 1970 vehicle had the narrow two-leaf door (which can be seen through the screens) and 47 full coach seats inside its body. Wheel trims and National coach livery completed what admittedly were fine vehicles.

a little help from the Chairman of her party whose well publicised affair brought about far reaching and unscheduled changes in the cabinet and in particular the appointment of her disciple Nicholas Ridley as Transport Secretary. The first target was Leyland and its sundry activities. Vast quantities of public funds had been poured into Leyland (cars) over many years and Thatcher's simple view was to stop the largesse, whatever the consequences. How did not come into the equation, and therefore when Ian McKinnon, Managing Director of parent Leyland Bus, offered a paltry £4 million for a business capitalised at £17 million (and allegedly having substantial amounts of uninvoiced finished stock!) a deal was struck. Just for good measure the Government also wrote off accumulated debts worth £55 million. McKinnon's proposal also included the proviso that he did not want this coach builder somewhere on the east coast. He had neither understood its business thus far nor did he intend to start now. He would however take with him the jigs and rights in the products just in case!

Such was the Government's determination to be rid of Leyland that these proposals went ahead with all speed. Two things are worth recalling when considering what chance the coach works stood amongst these events. Firstly, McKinnon sold Leyland Bus to Volvo within 18 months for a figure generally reckoned to be between £24-27 million. There was insufficient time or demand to turn its fortunes round on a diminishing market especially when that hungry cuckoo – Workington – was laying claim to such food as was to be found in the nest. One conclusion only can be drawn about the Government's zeal in securing the best terms for the country, that it was absolutely desperate to see the back of Leyland "at any price".

Secondly, it should not be forgotten that the parallel disposal of the car business was ultimately shown to have involved substantial 'illegal' aid to the buyer, British Aerospace, which had to be repaid.

Deregulation

The Government had embarked upon a first stage in its fundamental change in the licensing system for bus operation with coach deregulation in 1980, and Nicholas Ridley proposed to go headlong into full deregulation at the earliest opportunity. Simultaneously he proposed the break up of the National Bus Company into small companies – sometimes of dubious viability.

There was negligible consultation and it is highly doubtful if Ridley troubled himself to even acknowledge the existence of opposition let alone to consider it. His plans became law in the Transport Act of 1985. Thereafter vehicle orders ceased to be placed. Managers about to be forced to face competition, whilst at the same time having to convince bankers of the worth of their enterprises, fought shy of taking the burden of fleets of new buses into their companies.

Indeed there was an effective moratorium on investment in the industry from 1985 until virtually 1992/3 whilst each sector of the operating industry was sold into private ownership. This was the catalyst which deprived the coach works and most other bodybuilders of work. It should not be forgotten that ECW was not alone. MCW was an early casualty, Northern Counties was forced into administrative receivership and Duple was taken over by arch rival Plaxton in this period. Alexander too reduced its workforce and was sold to its management. They, however, at least had the comfort of so many years assiduous courtship of the Hong Kong body market by Ray Braithwaite which would stand them in good stead.

Inevitable?
No!

There were many opportunities for the coach works, had the consistent aim of Leyland Bus not been to save Workington. It would have been possible to have loaded both Bristol chassis plant and ECW fully and profitably with products they were capable of building, had there been the political will at Leyland to grasp the nettle of Workington in 1980. That plant was developed to build one (allegedly low cost) product under the artificial market created by a Government ultimately paying the operator 50% of his investment price for each bus. When that stopped so too did the need for the existence of the plant in question. Indeed the issue of the cost of the Leyland National is one to explore, as overall it did not turn out to be a cheap vehicle over its whole life. The ill-judged move

into assembling diesel multiple units for British Rail merely created excess capacity in that area also, apparently without creating a business with even short-term viability.

Did Leyland Bus misjudge the minibus market and its growth? That seems doubtful. It is more likely that they did not conceive that ECW could have contributed because they were quite blind to the possibility and set their policy against it. There was some effort to market complete large vehicles to operators in the 'eighties but a combination of bad luck over the Thailand deal and the superior efforts and will power of others put paid to this.

Buyout?

A combination of factors made this less likely than even at Optare/Charles Roe. Firstly ECW's way was long that of the gentleman, and senior people were getting close to retirement, Secondly no Plant Director or similar figure was still in place to take this forward when control was passed to the Rover Group in 1986. Optare had had two years start on ECW and the market had contracted to a

Non-NBC sales were later controlled by Leyland. This meant that salesmen who had little or no direct knowledge of the plant or its products reflected Leyland's policy for the plant rather than its capability. Arguably this was satisfactory whilst full order books were at hand – but the adage 'don't have all yours eggs in the one basket' was ignored. Northampton was however favoured by being permitted to have some LHs to go with the VRTs it was taking. KBD 21V leaves no one in any doubt as to its fleet number.

Jim Prior was the MP for Lowestoft at the time of the Titan debacle. He was one of Margaret Thatcher's 'wetter' colleagues but too important within her party to be peremptorily sacked.

Ian Bannochie McKinnon, the final Managing Director of Leyland Bus whose decision not to seek work for the factory in the minibus boom partially led to its not being included in his buyout plan.

"You shall wither on the vine" – Ken McIver

The loyalty and dedication which was extended to the company by its workforce is typified by the illustration below, reproduced from the Lowestoft Journal of 29th July 1977. Bill Blowers, seen on the right, progress controller for ECW, is receiving his retirement presents from Sid Wright, then factory manager. Bill had achieved a record no one could better – he had clocked up 51 years service since starting with United as the office boy, and then moving to the bodyshop. He went to Irthlingborough during the war, and on return to Lowestoft joined the inspection department. He transferred to works progress in 1962. It was that sort of long service which put ECW where it was, with a substantial hard core of its work force knowing every manufacturing trick in the book, together with first-hand experience of the individual needs of all its customers. Those who believe that there is no place in modern industry for such 'old fashioned' practices should ask themselves how often they come up against companies whose staff know nothing about their specific requirements, or possible long-relationship with that supplier? And if Leyland's policy of appointing top people who knew nothing about the industry was such a good idea, how come none of them lasted more than a mere fraction of Mr Blower's time?

Thirteen

What Might Have Been

ECW and its sister chassis manufacturer, Bristol Commercial Vehicles, had risen to the forefront of PSV Technology in the post-war period. Although never in the vanguard of the styling movement ECW bodies had developed an enviable reputation.

Even in what outwardly appeared to be the standardised 'fifties and 'sixties the company was preparing derivatives of its standard designs for those few areas into which it was able to sell. Primarily this meant northern municipal fleets where the British Railways Board had interests. Proposals were made to both the Sheffield and Huddersfield Joint Omnibus Committees, although with limited success.

With the RE family of body and chassis introduced in 1962 a market had been laid for single-decks which was to last for a long time. However, Bristol and ECW were looking at their options in how to approach the newly emergent 11m chassis length. Mid and rear engined underfloor designs were considered for both single AND double-decked vehicles. Clearly it was necessary to move to the stage of 'cutting metal' and the 'N' type chassis was developed and promised to be even more spectacular and to present the opportunity for what would have proved to be the bus equivalent of a clan of chassis! The basic concept was a chassis with a rear mounted longitudinal engine at the offside and a very low frame height. Thence by the expedient of varying the wheelbase it was proposed to produce the full range of vehicles required by the modern fleet of the day. This would have been an achievement only recently achieved (badly) by the Volvo B9M, B10M and D10M with their second cousin the B10B. The project had started slowly with drawings being produced by both companies for some of the variants. It is known that Bristol had built an 11m low frame chassis by 1965 but it is doubtful whether that ever left Brislington. Certainly by the spring of 1966, this had been reconstructed into the chassis which was numbered VRX001, receiving body EX 10 and subsequently being registered GGM 431D. However, events overtook the project, despite there being the suggestion of firm orders for 60 vehicles for Crosville Motor Services for operation on the newly designed Runcorn Busway. The events were of course Standard Bus Grant which had no place for double-deckers other than the rear transverse engined type, and the beginning of the take-over by Leyland which left the two companies to concentrate on more conventional products. The drawings show the range that had been envisaged at this time.

Later on the company tendered for various orders and although many of these were merely for variants of the standard products on either standard chassis – or even the like of the AEC Swifts for Great Yarmouth and Lowestoft – some were decidedly more unusual. When the death knell was sounding tenders were submitted both at home and abroad ranging from the Dennis Domino – probably for the South Yorkshire PTE as well as Volvo B10M Citybuses. In the event Leyland control – financial as well as political – probably stifled this endeavour and only Olympian demonstrators for various markets were actually built. It must be left to the imagination what an ECW body on a Leyland DAB articulated bus chassis might have looked like! – certainly rather more satisfying than the 'Leyland National on stilts' that forms the best description of the vehicles sold to South Yorkshire and British Airways.

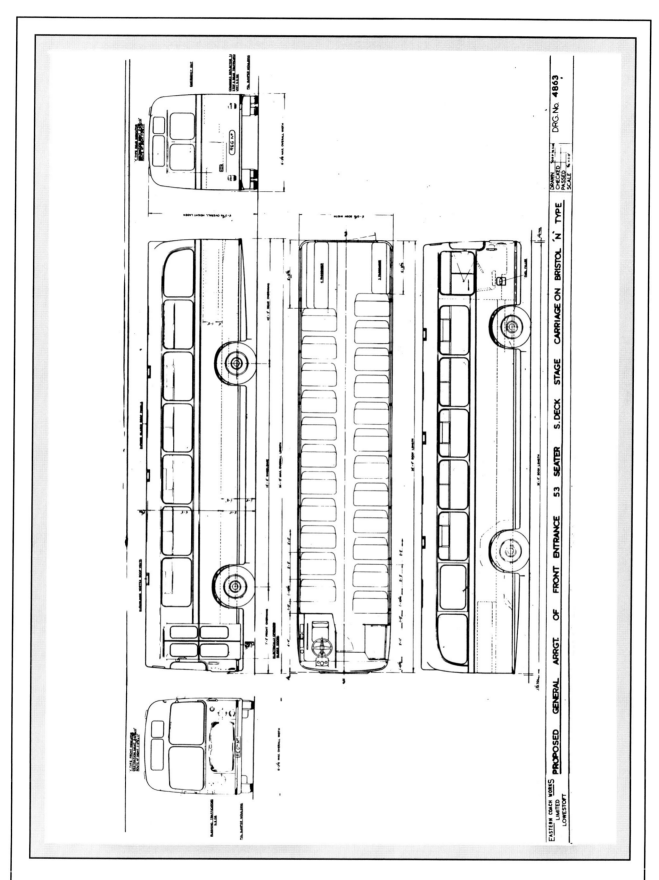

Drawing number 4863 dated 13th July 1965 shows the most conventional member of the N type clan. An 11m fully-seated single-decker – the equivalent of the Bristol RELL. There is provision shown for four passengers to sit over the engine and to permit the Emergency Exit to be in the back wall , the nearside rearmost seat is also longitudinal. A narrow front door is fitted and the styling is generally that of the contemporary RELL body then in production.

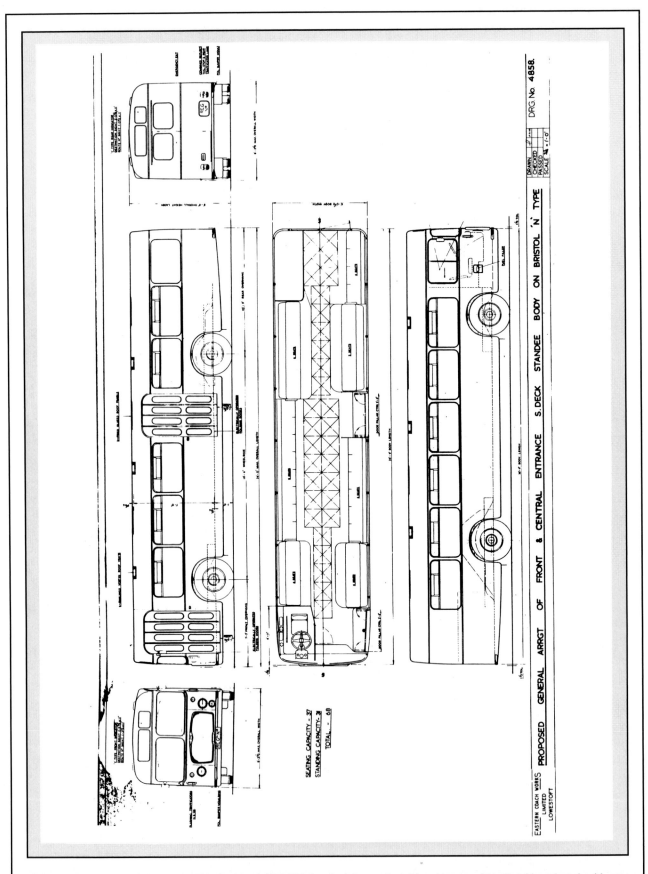

A slightly earlier drawing (4th June 1965) is numbered 4858. This is a dual-door variant: it is not too surprising that this variant should come first as there was much interest in the European concept of having everyone stand rather than sit for their journey. This latter is borne out by the perimeter seating for a mere 37 passengers – a further 31 being invited to stand. To allow for the anticipated need for speedier boarding and alighting wider doors were proposed. At about this time ECW had built two dual-doored Bristol MWs for Eastern Counties and were to build two dual-doored vehicles on REs to exhibit at the 1966 Commercial Motor Show. The principal styling feature which appeared to have been removed by July was the squared up rear dome although this might have owed more to the desire to make the interior less claustrophobic.

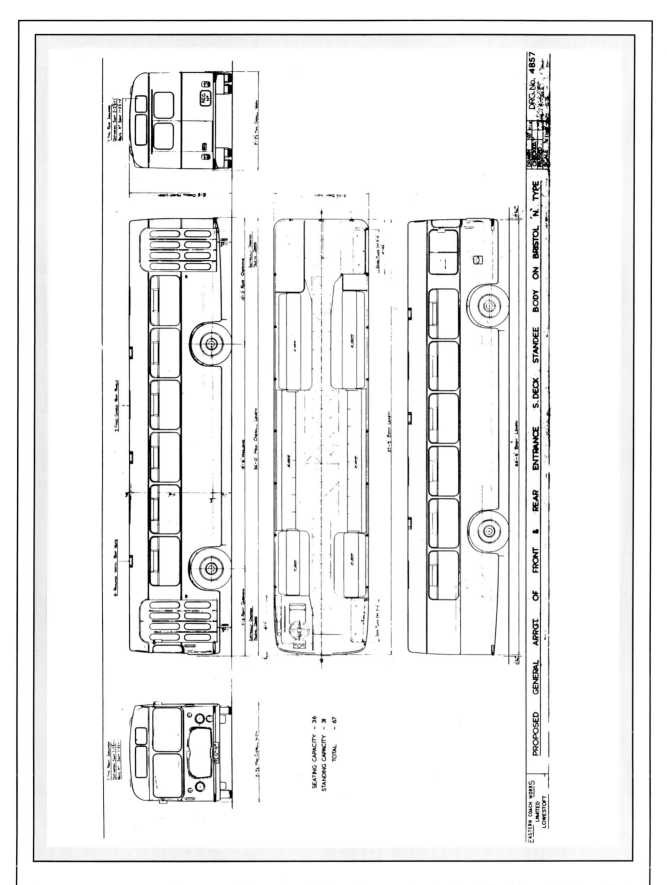

SEATING CAPACITY - 36
STANDING CAPACITY - 31
TOTAL - 67

EASTERN COACH WORKS LIMITED LOWESTOFT | PROPOSED GENERAL ARRGT. OF FRONT & REAR ENTRANCE S. DECK STANDEE BODY ON BRISTOL 'N' TYPE | DRG. No. 4857

The most avant guarde drawing of all was 4857 of January 1965. This showed the rear exit permitted by the chassis layout. Again the emphasis was on the flirtation with standing passengers. It was this version that was suggested for Crosville MS. However that company's first two vehicles for Runcorn Busway services were two Bristol RELL6G built with bodies with only 30 seats but upseated to 36 prior to entry to service. Following these proposals most operators reverted to vehicles which were substantially fully seated and had only one door. Even the Runcorn busway took 48 seaters for its first squadron of vehicles and later single-doored vehicles became the norm even there.

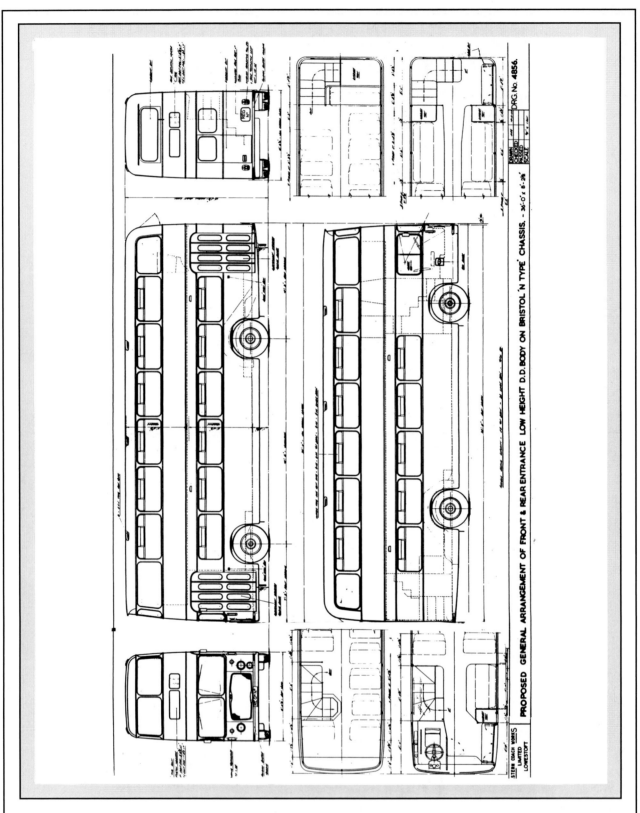

The extreme rear exit theme was continued on a drawing (4856 – 18th June 1965) which showed an 11m body for a low frame double-deck chassis – possibly the one which had been assembled at Bristol. The most notable features of this vehicle are the use of the curved glasses for the windscreens of both decks and PEAKED front dome. The use of the curved glasses is clearly related to the two existing RE variants but the peaked dome gives a clue to Stan George's thinking for the future. In the event the curved glasses clearly carried forward to the Ribble double-deck coach fleet whose first member was built in 1968 (on the only production variant of the N type by now christened the VRL) and the peaked domes were used on the RE by 1967 although the extravagant use of curved glass was dropped to ease the burden of widening the front door without lengthening the vehicle. That comment, of course, belies the fact that the RE body was later lengthened to accommodate curved glasses to reduce the night-time reflections in the flat variant. The overall height of the bus was proposed at 13ft 4½in – the height of the Lodekka. The vast bulk of production VRTs were to 13ft 8in height. The implication from a study of the drawing must be that the production chassis was higher as no evidence is shown of a sunken gangway etc. The traditional tapered front is shown and the space over the engine is usefully used for the second staircase. Eighty-one seats are shown.

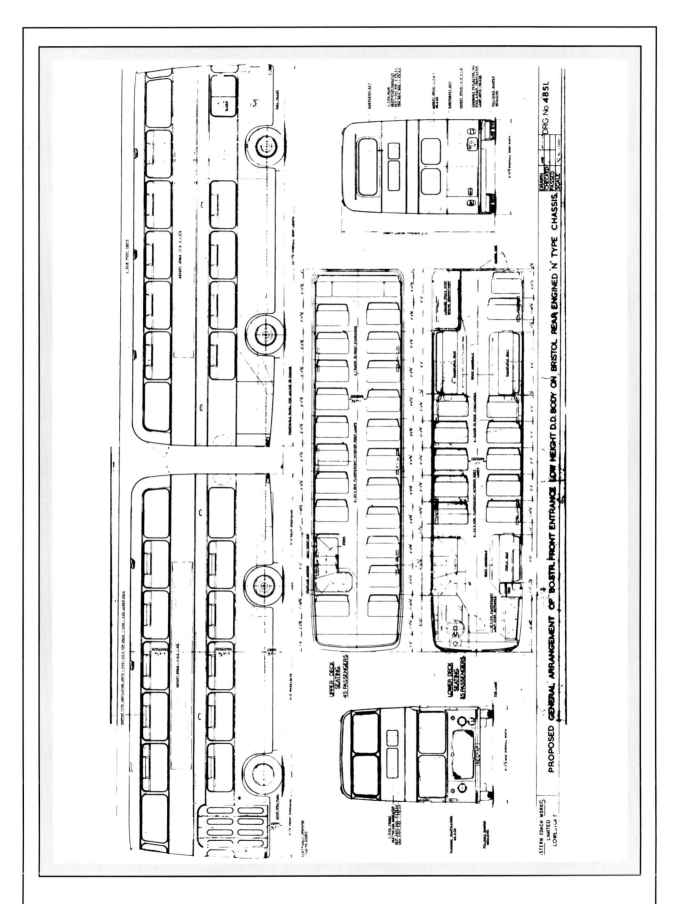

The only version to be produced – and then only for two vehicles – was the 10-metre 80-seat single-doored bus. Drawing 4851 from January 1965 is substantially that of the two VRX bodies although the curved glasses were supplanted by flat glass and the peaks deleted in favour of parts similar to the FLF Lodekka. The RE style front radiator grille was replaced by a new design.

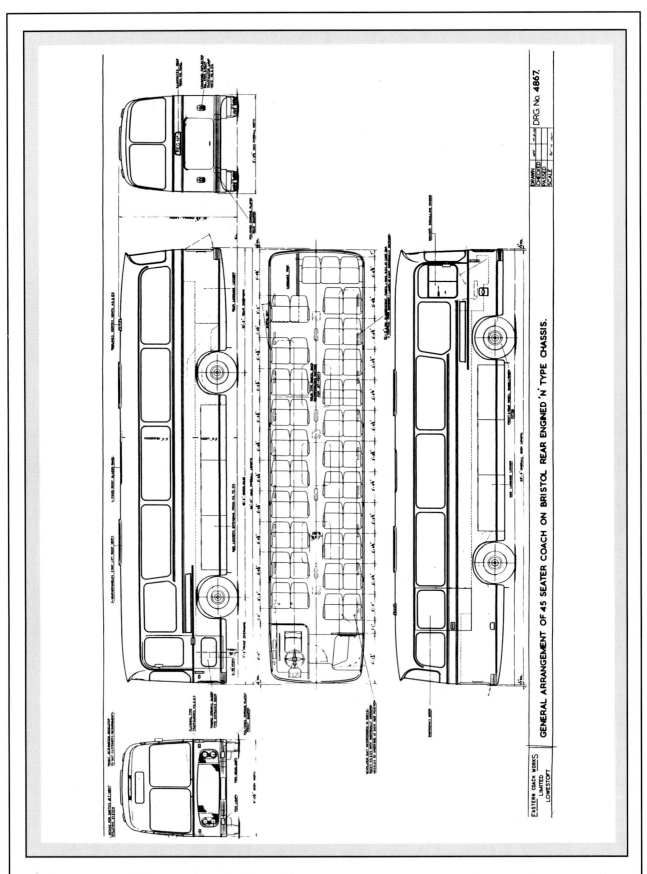

GENERAL ARRANGEMENT OF 45 SEATER COACH ON BRISTOL REAR ENGINED 'N' TYPE CHASSIS.

EASTERN COACH WORKS
LIMITED
LOWESTOFT

DRG. No. 4867.

Two drawings exist (4655 and 4867 – 15th and 14th May 1965 respectively) for the coach member of the clan proposed for the Tilling Group's extensive Express Service commitments. Naturally enough a flat floor was proposed for the saloon with opportunity to install extensive underfloor lockers for luggage. To facilitate this a higher through chassis was envisaged. Two styling proposals existed. The styling of 4867 is interesting in that it envisages a stepped window line with front and rear screens common – but opposite ways up! A clever yet effective move although the side view of the rear end is not unlike Harrington lines of the time. Peaks have crept in at the front and the two drawings imply that there was some doubt as to the intended location of the radiator in production.

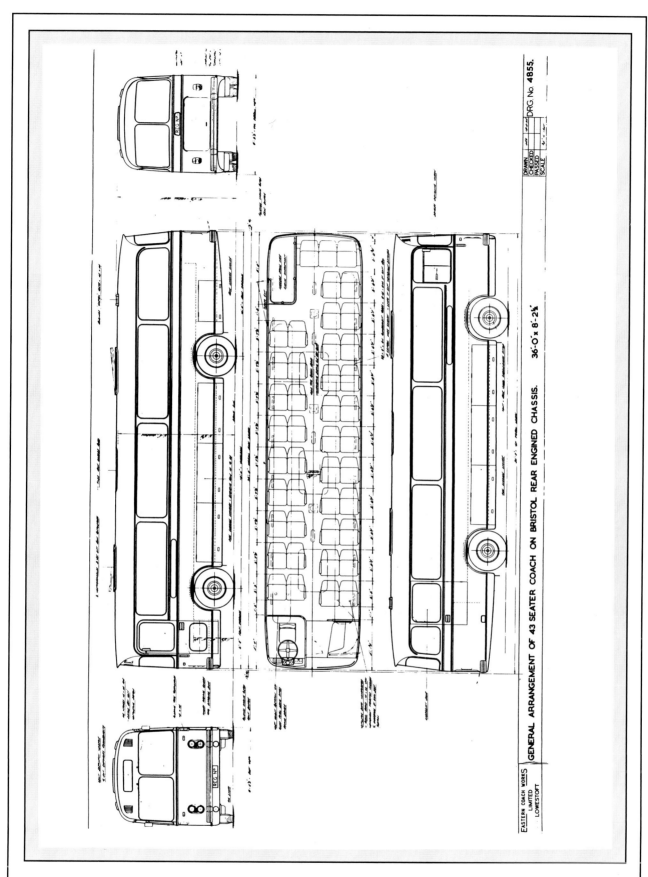

Drawing 4867 shows a front mounting with body styling of the existing Mark 1 RE coach body yet 4855 clearly shows a plain unstyled front. Drawing 4855 also shows a waistline similar to the existing coach body and although curved glasses were envisaged (possibly of the bus pattern) these were common to each end once more. Bumpers of the existing RE pattern were shown. Variable seating capacities were shown for the 11m vehicle although the largest – at 45 – would seem unconscionably low and thus uneconomic even by ECW's quest for luxury. The 43-seat variation would have suited both United and Eastern National both then good customers for the RELH coach.

Above: Even toward the end there was experimental work under way and these pictures show the scope of some of it. One set of vehicles which did not get much beyond the frame stage were those intended for export territories. The extent of work on Leyland chassis 8300829 is shown on page 120/121 of ECW 1965-87. This is a sketch of how the finished product was intended to look. This really was quite attractive and in typical fashion used many standard parts. From the waist rail upwards, roof included, much of the structure was that of the 13ft 8in Olympian.

Below: A prototype set of body parts was built up to develop a CKD body for the Far East. The exercise was numbered EX25 and was substantially completed. Brian Wright took this photograph in the Experimental shop. The exercise came to nothing – probably because of Leyland's lack of interest – and the shell was dismantled without a chassis ever being allocated for it.

Fourteen

Building an Olympian

The influence of some of the outsiders has been demonstrated in the last few pages but numbered amongst the 'men' are the coachbuilders and others who worked in the factory. Some of the aspects of their daily operations will be seen in the following photographs.

The first Olympian body takes shape in the experimental area. EX17 became Ribble 2101 as the prototype for the National Bus Company. After several days struggling to get the body side to fit the slightly banana-shaped chassis the solution was found by jacking up the chassis with Accro props to enable it to fit the body side, rather than working the other way as had been intended.

After the experimental shop had successfully developed the concept, the body would have been 'productionised' to use modern parlance. The most economical methods of production and subsequent assembly would have been devised. That would have meant extensive negotiations within each 'shop' as the various stewards fought for the best rate they could achieve in their areas. This view shows a jig-built side for an NBC Olympian being carried by roof-mounted lifting gear to an assembly station. This was a radically different method of assembly from that previously encountered in the coach factory.

The side units are married to the chassis, intermediate roof and rear assembly. Much of the missing remainder (apart from the roof unit) would come together as the fibre glass components were incorporated.

A detail of the rear offside corner of a home market Olympian showing the Avdelok type rivets imported from the Leyland National and some of the general flimsiness which came from the northern plant. Compare the views on this page with the traditional methods shown earlier.

Erection completed! The difference in tones on the panels of this NBC shell show those areas moulded in glass fibre and those which are conventionally sheeted in aluminium. The use of glass fibre in itself is not criticised but those familiar with the construction of traditional ECW products and, dare one say, the Mark 1 Leyland National, cannot but see the pervading change of philosophy evident in these vehicles. The same was sadly evident in the B51.

A view in the paintshop with vehicles for Merseyside PTE on the right and an NBC Olympian on the left. It was unusual to find this shop partially empty, as here, and the photograph was taken after an internal dispute which had stopped production for some days.

A later view showing the final assembly area – in this instance rather too final, for the vehicles in sight are the last of the London Transport order which heralded the end of the coach factory's existence.

Appendix 1

Development Vehicles

Throughout its long life the company always sought to upgrade the product, whether it was in terms of improved life or functionality. Many individual vehicles incorporated such features as a matter of course. Starting with the first post-war L6A which, although destined to become Crosville KB1, was actually not delivered for 18 months after construction, this continued during the 'fifties and 'sixties. ECW produced a number of shells on prototype Bristol chassis which were then used by both companies for development purposes. Normally when this work was adjudged complete, the vehicle was brought up to service standard passed to one or another of the operating companies. Some of these can be seen in these pages.

1957 saw a revival of the development 'hack'. These two illustrations show the second MW chassis (135.002) and the body was produced to early erect rear outline with DP brightwork. It was later fitted out as a bus and passed to Red and White (the original Chepstow Company not the sept of the Stagecoach clan of today) as 228 JAX. Interestingly this vehicle was fitted with a Bristol BHW engine for a while. This was a 1958 development of Bristol's own engine having a one-piece cylinder block and crank case. Rated at 8.9 litres and around 105 BHP, it was not terribly successful although the need for its existence was perpetuated as Messrs L. Gardner and Son Limited (of Patricroft fame) the preferred supplier, still lived in a world where it decided what it would supply, to whom and when. That meant the chassis builder needed a secondary source to maintain production – in this case, in house. How times have changed with Gardner living on the brink of an abyss until very recently in 1995 when a massive order for LXB engines was secured from China – a country none too fussed about outdated technology.

1959/60 saw the Lodekka move forward to the FLF, in 30ft form although there was still one further development – the 31ft 6in chassis – to follow rather later. The recently-revived practice of having a development chassis was continued and ECW provided this unfitted shell (12009) on FLF6B 169.001. The vehicle was fitted out for service use in 1967, and delivered to Eastern Counties in the April of that year as LAH 448E. It retained many of its 1960 characteristics but also some of its experimental features. The vehicle passed to Top Deck Travel afterwards for their long haul holidays across the world. As this book closes the vehicle still lies, nearly complete, in the yard of PVS at Barnsley.

Another development vehicle seen in 1966. Bristol RELH chassis REX003 was prepared for BCV use. Again this vehicle was fitted with the BHW engine for a while, although it found no more favour than before, and was shortly to be dropped from production even in the BVM form required to sustain Lodekka production in the face of Gardner's imperial *hauteur* – probably to the relief of many chief engineers. This vehicle was refitted as a coach and sent to West Yorkshire Road Car where it spent a full life as a front line vehicle.

1966 saw the completion of RELL chassis 3/101. This was equipped with air suspension and many advanced features. Although used for development purposes it also saw much use as a demonstrator – and was singularly successful in notching up sales. Painted caramel and cream it was unusual in being sold to the Road Transport Industry Training Board, firstly at High Ercall then at Livingstone. It is believed to have been scrapped some years ago.

Another vehicle whose purpose was demonstration as well as development was NHU 100F, the first LH (001) with Perkins engine. This was finished in Tilling Green and after a less successful demonstration life, passed to Eastern Counties for service use. At that time the front dome was modified as described elsewhere in this book.

131

Appendix 2

Production Figures 1927-42

YEAR	S/D	D/D	LORRIES/VANS	TOTAL
1927	273	NIL	2	275
1928	255	NIL	NIL	255
1929	213	NIL	7	220
1930	177	NIL	NIL	177
1931	56	20	14	90
1932	153	50	6	209
1933	183	49	2	234
1934	336	22	NIL	358
1935	453	73	NIL	526
1936	505	43	NIL	548
1937	552	106	NIL	658
1938	461	240	NIL	701
1939	400	198	NIL	598
1940	203	143	NIL	346
1941	31	29	NIL	60
1942	39	9	NIL	48

The above information was extracted from records compiled by Maurice Doggett.
Information for the years prior to 1927, in United days, is incomplete and information for
the wartime period is also incomplete. Post-war production statistics will be found in
Venture's ECW History covering the period 1946-65, or its later volume covering 1965-87.

During the 'sixties one of two small chassis types bodied was the Bristol SU. Not a very refined basis for a coach perhaps but this quite neat body was produced using many standard components, an ongoing virtue of Coach Factory designs when dealing with low volume yet essential variants of the standard product. Most of these vehicles went to Western/Southern National, but two, of which 753 BWN is seen here, went to United Welsh.

Appendix 3

The Legal Framework

Eastern Coach Works Limited was formed on 1st July 1936 to carry on the body building business of Eastern Counties Omnibus Company Limited. It was incorporated as company number 315856. The capital subscribed was £100,000, in cash, in respect of £1 ordinary shares. This in turn had been the continuation of the body building business of United Automobile Services Limited.

The initial shareholders comprised:

Eastern Counties OC Ltd	24,400 shares
Ribble MS Ltd	37,600 shares
Thos. Tilling Ltd	37,600 shares
East Midland MS Ltd	100 shares
East Yorks MS Ltd	100 shares
	99,800

There were also nominal small holdings of 100 shares each by E Bennett Esq and R J Ellery Esq to facilitate their positions on the Board. Numbered amongst the Directors were John Frederick Heaton, John Spencer Wills and William Spencer Wreathall – three of the 'Great and the Good' of the day. The composition reflected joint Tilling and BET influence which was to last until 1942. The capitalisation was increased to £800,000 in 1953, the final figure during the life of the coach works.

Nationalisation in 1948 had brought the shares under the ownership of the British Transport Commission. They were further transferred, upon the reorganisation of state transport interests, to the Transport Holding Company in 1962 when the various businesses of BTC were separated.

The next change came at the behest of the Labour Government in 1965 to circumvent the restriction in sales incorporated into the nationalisation legislation. At this time, 25% of the shares were transferred to the Leyland Motor Corporation in 1965 in exchange for just under 30% of Park Royal Vehicles. This gave both ECW and Bristol Commercial Vehicles what today would be termed 'Associated Company' status and thus they could draw on the rights of the new shareholder.

Red and White was a late convert to ECW products, but some of its rebodyings produced interesting combinations such as Albions with post-war bodies. This very typical Bristol MW is seen with three-piece destination, cream rubber glazing gasket and, to judge by the unpainted wheel-nuts, was photographed when virtually new.

Men from the North

The Transport Act of 1968 created the National Bus Company and on vesting date 1st January 1969, the shares held by THC were duly transferred to it. Shortly afterwards Leyland and the fledgling NBC entered into the Leyland National deal by which they would jointly produce the vehicle for which Leyland had hitherto found little enthusiasm. Inevitably the creation of new capacity in the manufacturing sector was going to alter the market place quite dramatically and the ramifications of this were the basis for the justification of National Bus stepping back from management control of its erstwhile in-house manufacturers.

The mechanism for the changes perceived to be required was Bus Manufacturers Holdings Ltd which had a share capital of £6000 divided equally between the two, and in turn held all but one (NBC) of the shares in ECW. The split of shares was slightly unusual:–

National Bus Company	2999
British Leyland Truck and Bus	2000
National Bus Nominees Ltd	1
British Leyland International Ltd	1000

The involvement of NBNL was a continuation of THC practice, for secretarial purposes, (the company previously being called THC Nominees) and BLI was to recognise that body's role in exports at the time. Unfortunately BLI was quite reasonably known amongst some at Leyland as 'Blight' for its devastating effect on anything it touched. The operating subsidiaries were to be ECW, British Commercial Vehicles, Park Royal Vehicles, Charles H Roe and a new entity, Leyland National Ltd, which ran the Workington plant. The significant point of this change was the Bus Manufacturers Holdings Ltd was a Leyland management company and whose chairman was a Leyland nominee. Leyland had now wrested management control from NBC and Ron Ellis duly succeeded Tony Gailey of NBC as Chairman of ECW on 16th September 1969.

A sick partner

British Leyland's shareholding of course became bound up in the collapse of that company and was later controlled via the National Enterprise Board. However, in its dying days in 1974/5 the original British Leyland reorganised Bus Manufacturers Holdings Ltd. At this time the thrust of corporate management had changed so far as both BCV and ECW were concerned. It was now the case that the two plants were already pawns in the greater game of chess which Leyland survival was to become. Those who are familiar with the tactics of chess will, of course, recollect that a skilled player will, from time to time, sacrifice certain useful players for the greater good of a strategy.

This was to become quite important less than ten years later ...

In the meantime ECW Ltd ceased to trade as a separate company, the undertaking and assets passing to Leyland National Limited, which, to confuse matters, renamed itself Bus Manufacturers Ltd. Also transferred were the assets and undertakings of the other companies in this

This VRT is not all it seems. Firstly, to state the obvious, HWJ 924W did not belong to West Yorkshire – rather it was on loan from Yorkshire Traction for use on the York City Tour. Its use was said to be in the nature of an experiment but something clearly caught on for today York seems to have a squadron of open-toppers. Secondly, it had not been built as an open-topper but as a normal vehicle. Following an accident with a low bridge Tracky converted it into what became the 53rd convertible VRT, using parts purchased from ECW. (Open-toppers 1-50 were built at Lowestoft, 51 and 52 were converted by National Welsh and 54 is under conversion at Northern Bus in Sheffield.) Curiously Road Car, a subsidiary of Traction, have now converted it back to a normal vehicle using parts from a withdrawn example.

grouping. Bus Manufacturers Holdings Ltd continued to exercise ownership as before over the reorganised businesses.

It was at this time that the famous ECW oval trade mark changed for the first and only time: the work 'Limited' disappeared, affecting all vehicles fitted out after 1st January 1975.

Many will wonder at the reasons behind such manoeuvres at a time when British Leyland was very much a sinking ship. Up to then ECW had been organised and managed as any other limited company and that would impose certain duties upon the directors, and also make its financial affairs relatively transparent. Now it was being managed simply as a manufacturing out-post of a large corporation without the stewardship of a Board of Directors promoting its interest and marking its successes. No longer would the efforts of its workers necessarily be the significant factor in its retention. However successful it might be, closure could follow if another corporate objective was deemed more important by those at the centre. That did not bode well for a business which was likely to be thought to be expendable by a remote head office – even of its own family division.

It is very difficult to avoid the conclusion that the reason was to mingle the Workington plant's ongoing losses into the profits of ECW and BCV and at the same time make them more difficult to trace. At the same time NBC personnel would cease to have direct representation at plant level at either BCV or ECW, reducing to virtually nil their input to management. Leyland were more firmly in control on a day-to-day basis. A stark contrast to the days, not many years before, when interviews for even middle management posts were held at the Head Office of a bus operating group – by the directors of the operating companies.

In controlling any company or group of companies, it is inevitable that the bigger the group, the less influence the Directors have, as so much can be left aside as 'plant level detail' or a 'day-to-day management' matter. Plant directors can easily be excluded from such exalted circles as well. That simplistic view does little justice to NBC representatives on the board, but it happens to be the position into which they were manoeuvred by Leyland – with possibly not a little help from the government of the day, which was undoubtedly anxious to do anything which could reduce the drain upon the public purse of the Leyland group. In fairness to NBC it has to be said that the company was facing its own significant operating problems from a hostile Department of Transport and was not the efficient enterprise which Malcolm (Lord) Shepherd and Robert Brook subsequently created. Undoubtedly it was not in a position to publicly denounce any changes – even had it so wished.

The shares in the by then dormant Eastern Coach Works Limited were held by Bus Manufacturers Ltd. In 1982 National Bus Company sold its interests in Bus Manufacturers Holdings Limited to its notional partner, Leyland Vehicles Ltd, which had assumed the BL share in one of the many reorganisations. The reason stated was that NBC could no longer justify diverting its efforts to an unrelated activity and one which was making a loss. The latter was not without its problems, however, which were to have an effect on the coach works. What was not said publicly at the time was that National Bus was now being forced to fight for its own life. Following the success of the Privatisation of the National Freight Corporation the Department of Transport was looking at disposing of NBC – a 50% holding in a Leyland subsidiary would certainly have been viewed as an encumbrance – as indeed it would have been under Ridley's ultimate plan. With transfer went the coach factory's key allies – the operators.

The Eastern Counties transfer applied externally to the vehicles was itself based on the original United design, using an oval shape with gold leaf. Eastern Coach Works also used an oval, but they decided to apply it to the inside of the vehicles on the basis that it would last longer before being overpainted. From 1936 when the design was introduced until the end of production, there was only one change to the design, implemented from 1st January 1975, when the word 'Limited' was deleted.

Sight of contemporary management papers makes very clear that neither ECW or Bristol were the culprits in creating the loss which was of concern to NBC.

Some Statistics for the time

	Turnover	Profit	
ECW 1980	£14,528m	£2,761m	19.0%
ECW 1981	£12,665m	£1,64m	12.9%
BCV 1980	£21,609m	£1,923m	8.9%
BCV 1981	£24,421m	£1,402m	5.7%
Workington 1980	£28,587m	(£0.256m)	

Notes

- 1981 figures are actuals to end September plus the period ten updated forecast.
- Profits are stated before interest and Tax. Figures in parentheses are of course losses.
- (a) The reduced figure for ECW resulted from short time working in the autumn because of delays in chassis supply from Bristol. This in turn was due to delays in introducing the Olympian to build through industrial relations problems which arose from a threat of redundancies in the BCV machine shops. The cause was the machining hitherto undertaken at the plant on VRT components would cease as Leyland's custom was for Farington to undertake such work on components designed at that site. Yet another example of corporate culture wreaking havoc at what was a peripheral site.
- (b) The comparatively poor 1981 at BCV and ECW is a result of the new model and the loss of the last 15% of run out, which generates a disproportionate part of the profit. At the same time labour for the higher level of output was on hand.

This sobering comparison was the underlying reason Leyland assumed full control of the ECW business by altering the legal structure of its existence. It was now entirely at the mercy of Leyland's fortunes and central objectives as described elsewhere in this volume. The Lowestoft plant could neither control nor indeed influence its ultimate fate. Indeed with certain key functions – selling and corporate planning dealt with by Leyland Bus, it was merely to build that which it was told to do. Plant directors of the period recall that the coach factory was not allowed to even have a sales brochure to extol its wares – it merely received a mention at the back of a Leyland Bus offering, headed 'We also make .....' The introduction or development of a new product was quite out of the question. This was to prove very significant in the dash to minibuses from 1984 onwards, a race into which ECW was not even entered by its masters.

The ECW company, it will be recalled, was still dormant at this time and it was not until 1986 that it was revived and renamed BUTEC Ltd, to acquire Leyland's in-house electrical component department and give that company status in anticipation of a sale. Leyland Vehicles had formally taken control of the shares in 1983. The renamed company was sold in 1987.

Although the detail of the story is recorded elsewhere it is poignant to recall that Paul Channon, Secretary of State for Industry, announced the closure of the business of Eastern Coach Works in the House of Commons on 24th July 1986. This was 50 years and 24 days from its inception. Little wonder that no Golden Jubilee celebrations had been planned.

Let not the Scots be forgotten!

A drab Glasgow the backcloth to a long FLF of Central SMT. BL292 (FGM 292D) seated 76 with additional provision for luggage as seen through the window behind the stairs. The vehicle has the 1966 design of updated body.

Northern General provided a show exhibit for ECW in 1975 with this early Mark 3 VRT, the dual-door variant was not very well laid out downstairs – largely because of the various floor levels associated with the lowheight body.

ECW was given the job of completing to coach standards the Roe bodies for West Yorkshire PTE since the contract was incomplete at the time that the Leeds factory was about to be closed by Leyland. it later reopened under the Optare banner.

Appendix 4 Patents

Whilst patents may seem a dry aspect of the business they can be very revealing in some instances. The following Patents were granted jointly to the company and the individuals named. The law of Patents has developed greatly since that period and at the time the name of the employee did not confer any substantial benefit. The role of the individual in actually developing the idea should be viewed with some reserve, especially where that individual is the overall plant manager.

Patent	Date of Appn	Date of grant	Applicants
557556	19. 05. 42	25.11.43	ECW Ltd and W. Bramham
Improvements in body construction in relation to strength and weight control: Relates to new bodies from October 1942.			

Patent	Date of Appn	Date of grant	Applicants
562395	24.12.42	29.06.44	ECW Ltd and W. Bramham
Resilient glazing gasket in which the edges of the glass were embedded and which formed a cushion between the edges of the glass and the surrounding walls of the window opening. Incorporated in production from late 1942.			

One of two significant Patents. This provided for the style of glazing which was to serve to the end of VRT production in 1981. The significance of the ease of glazing and the security of the glass which it conferred has never been bettered. To recognise this it is only necessary to look at Park Royal style products where an external metal plate has to be employed or Alexander and MCW-bodied vehicles which require that the rubber glazing gasket be rivetted to the vehicles in vulnerable uses.

Patent	Date of Appn	Date of grant	Applicants
627986	09.08.46	19.08.46	ECW Ltd and W. Bramham
Design of sliding window which could readily be removed from the slideways without dismantling the window assembly. This was incorporated from early 1947 and was extended to cover doors and panels.			

Visually this is a most significant feature of ECW production 1947 to 1982 as it represented the ECW 'Top Slider' opening window vent. Frequently copied when the Patent ran out, yet no competitor ever achieved the elegance of this mundane yet essential feature.

Patent	Date of Appn	Date of grant	Applicants
637874	15.05.47	31.05.50	ECW Ltd and W. Bramham
An improvement over the earlier Patent 557556 and yet one which unusually merited the grant of Patent in its own right, whereby the longitudinal members of the body structure were inserted into and passed through passages formed for this purpose in the upright members/pillars and secured by any preferred means of fastening the longitudinal members to the upright ones.			

Top: An early Lodekka body plate. Due to the close collaboration between Bristol and ECW on this semi integral vehicle a 'joint' plate was used.

Centre: Later on reference to BTC was omitted and when the Motor Constructional (sic) Works (as it was known at Bristol) and Bristol's bus operations were split that name changed also.

Lower: London Transport was wont to be different in everything associated with its fleet and ECW's body plate used on the GS vehicles.respected that convention.

The crucial Patent. It was from this base point that the strength of the ECW body was derived alongside its unsurpassed crash resistance, oft said to be some latterday advance. The concept was pursued further by Stan George when he designed the body structure for the LS bus. The extrusion which *inter alia* formed the waist rail carried the principle to its logical conclusion. These two factors acting together mean that ECW can be credited with creating a 'system' of bodybuilding which can only rival (twenty years before) that of Alusuisse. An example of the United Kingdom leading the world and failing to secure recognition for it. It is thought possible that Bramham may have used the patent method in bodies produced at Northern Coach Builders after his move there.

A complete curiosity was that body plates referring to this patent carried the number 637674 which was actually in respect of coin feed automatic gramophones. ('Jukeboxes'!)

Patent	Date of Appn	Date of grant	Applicants
659902	28.01.49	31.10.51	A. J. Romer (ECW) F. J. Buswell

This relates to the original (BTCC) and Bristol Tramways Lodekka and Carriage Co Ltd body design for the Lodekka chassis whereby a reduction in height was achieved whilst maintaining the conventional seating layout of a normal height double-deck bus.

Another very significant Patent when coupled with 638426 granted to BTCC in respect of the transmission layout of the two prototype Lodekkas registered LHY 949 and JWT 712. In part this explains why the rest of the bus building industry was forced to sit back and watch until the Patent protection ran out after ten years. A subsequent Patent (698895) granted to BTCC and its employees E H Dine and F J Buswell (how apt!) covered the production layout of the Lodekka transmission (Appn 07.12.50, granted 28.10.53) to secure this advance for the two Tilling Group partners. Had it not been for the burden of nationalisation it would have been extremely interesting to have seen the take up of the Lodekka in the rest of the UK. Given the closeness of the UK specification to the European height limit of 4 metres, what export potential might Bristol have exploited both in Europe and beyond? So far as is known the only licence to have been granted was to Dennis Brothers of Guildford in respect of their assembly of the 'Loline' which was in reality a rebadged Lodekka.

Other 'lookalikes' such as the Brislington Body Works (BBW) and Brighton Hove & District vehicles are known to have been constructed with parts supplied by the coach factory. Apart from Northern Coach Builders whose special case is referred to elsewhere it can probably be safely assumed that a 'licence' was implied by the sales of the parts in question and that 'under the skin these vehicles were to their manufacturers standard specification'.

One factor which cannot be overlooked was that the Tilling Group had very strong views on what vehicles should look like – normally formed by the Lowestoft designers – and this would suggest that parts were supplied to achieve this uniformity of look. In BBW's case, of course, it is likely that virtually whole bodies were built from ECW parts or drawings.

Another general comment has to be the long term forethought of Bill Bramham in particular, the man who doubted the likelihood of a favourable outcome to the war, in securing the patents for ECW bodies when much of the country's mind was on 'the war effort'. This action certainly set up ECW in technical areas for the rest of its independent existence. Had it remained in the private sector, conjecture would suggest a pre-eminent if not dominant position in its industry could have been established.

Below left, upper and lower: Patents obviously had a limited life and the simplified plate for body 16446 reflects this. That for 19274 should show the loss of Limited Company status on 1st January 1975, but in fact is a duplicate plate specially made for the author's collection!

Below right upper: Towards the end of production Leyland introduced build numbers to comply with one of its systems and this number appeared on the body plate. This plate is historically significant being the one for the final vehicle (LT L263) photographed prior to fitment.

Below right lower: It is not unknown for hospitals to mix up the progeny in their maternity units. To prevent this happening in the Lowestoft storage yard, each incoming chassis was labelled with one of these plates which was wired to the steering column. It was not removed until delivery was imminent.

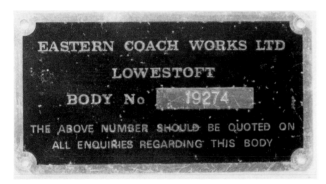

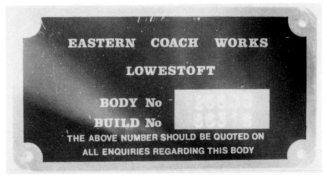

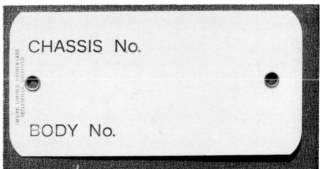

Appendix 5   The Premises

Eastern Way, and before that Laundry Lane, was a well-known and respected address in transport circles. For the enthusiast it was a Mecca. Where else could you walk along a public highway where the doors opened directly into the finishing shops, and where the vehicles were parked the right way round for photography every day of the year? The men at the Coach Factory must have been an amiable breed to cope with the attentions of the enthusiasts and public alike. Contrast this with the attitude adopted by many present-day railwaymen, for instance, who draw the blinds in their cabs lest anyone see them at work.

A view from the far end of the factory, by the railway level crossing. Note the name panels above the doors have been blacked out prior to the change of ownership to ECOC.

The other end of the complex showing the original brick office building and photographed at the time of take over by ECOC, doubtless as part of the valuation exercise.

A view taken towards the end of production and clearly illustrating for those who were never able to visit ECW just how accessible the factory and its vehicles really were. Now the whole area has been redeveloped as a retail shopping complex and the factory is but a memory.

The Last Round-up

Over the early 'fifties a number of oddities were produced – and none more so than this United vehicle – RHN 709 is a Guy Arab UF. At least the 5LW Gardner engine was common. Presumably this was a group evaluation exercise and so the vehicle remained a one-off, indeed the UF was hardly a best seller anywhere in the country.

Along with Commer and AEC-engined examples the Bristol LS body and chassis each appeared in a number of guises. Amongst the 1956 build was this later styled vehicle, one of ten delivered to Crosville in that year. It has never been satisfactorily explained and UG 331 featured bus seats in virtually a dual-purpose interior with chromed light fittings etc. The seats were, however, covered in a London Transport moquette not repeated in any order for the company or other Tilling Group subsidiary. The exterior was not that of the bus either – wrong waist moulding (a structural feature see chapter 11) and revised brightwork from a DP variant – but that selected by Crosville for the other eleven members of its batch. Does anyone in Lowestoft know the origins of this vehicle? Please let the author know for his forthcoming books on Crosville – that way another one of life's little mysteries can be resolved.

It must not be forgotten that others were equally guilty of producing 'disaster wagons' at this time and Willowbrook surely took all the medals with what became known, almost universally, as the 'Cardboard Leopard' although officially bestowed with the name 003 ! The placing of the order by NBC in 1978 was ordained by the then Labour Government of James Callaghan, Loughborough being a useful seat to win in the forthcoming General Election. Willowbrook's then owner George Hughes was passing about the Industry threatening to create hundreds of jobs in building buses for export – in Liverpool. This did not actually happen, but political conscience was little troubled by the reality of the proposal. These vehicles, apart from being badly put together slowly – for their intended delivery dates were exceeded by up to eighteen months and some were reallocated to Plaxton in desperation – suffered from leaking roofs, inadequate steel sections with no corrosion protection, and tissue paper thin glass fibre ends that any self-respecting bus wash could easily remove in one pass, amongst other failings. The 'design' input was even less, being but a poor clone of the early Duple Dominant. A very few were extensively rebuilt by NBC companies and others, and produced usable, if dreary, stage-carriage vehicles. Their use on better work was spasmodic even if essential for short periods when new.

Another instance of 'detachable' boots came with certain Marshall bodies to standard BET style. The problem, which came to light in a similar way to that of the B51, was dealt with quite effectively by recourse to the Aircraft Division at Marshalls whose knowledge of stress calculations was enormous. The common problem is that on mid-engined chassis with foreshortened frames to permit a boot, a 'cantilever' body is required ie the rear section is cantilevered from the middle frame. A lateral Stress Transfer Panel is thus required to put the loads into predetermined sections of the structure designed to cope. Thus if this fundamental is incorrectly provided, break up of the structure via its weakest point will surely ensue. Another problem which affected this type was inevitable on steel bodies. Corrosion which was quite severe – and premature – in many cases inevitably followed from the BET Group's reversion to steel structures as required by S G Vince, its Chief Engineer.

Returning to happier times in coachbuilding. ECW was always prepared to adapt its standard designs and this MW coach body was produced in 1960 for Tillings Travel but mounted on a second-hand AEC Regal chassis which had previously borne an ECW body to the LT RFW pattern! This 34-seater has an optional waistrail moulding and glazed front dome. Other modifications are the straight edge to the trailing edge of the door and the Bristol/ECW Wing Motif altered to show TT for Tilling Travel.

United Automobile always maintained a five-strong Extended Tours Fleet and some will remember the batch of LS6Bs produced in 1958 after the MW was in production. 1961's build continued to demonstrate this individuality and this 34-seater shows various non-standard features. Quite apart from the livery mouldings and lack of door kerb window, the draught deflectors over the side windows are a throw back to almost pre-war times, as is the solid dome with illuminated fleetname.

Strangely, United took another batch of touring coaches in 1962 which utilised the new body of that year. United's individuality is present – the brightwork below the windscreens is missing as is the kerb window. These survived in this role until 1970 when five Bristol LH/Plaxton Elites took over: the MWs then had a few years on Scarborough Tours before disposal.

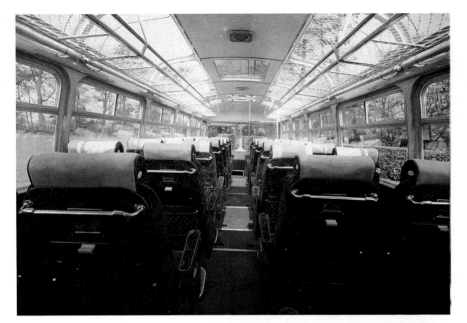

The United coaches seen on the previous page really were superbly appointed coaches for the day. Thirty-four reclining seats to ECW's sumptuously upholstered standard (probably on Chapman mechanisms), glove nets and even fold-down tables were incorporated. The latter features are scarcely fitted to modern coaches equipped with that scourge of the day – the 'Drinks Machine'. The stainless steel grab handles on the seats were doubtless useful to the elderly who would be predominant amongst the passengers, but their presence would not have enhanced safety. The open net coat racks and cantrail glazing provides for a light airy vehicle, ideal for sight seeing. Unfortunately the heating systems were not up to this amount of glass and some companies removed the roof glazing from 1962/3 build and they were then deleted from the specification.

ECW remained committed to maximising the appearance of its products and these two styling bucks appeared in 1972 to determine whether the side lamp units should be horizontal or vertical. The results are seen below.

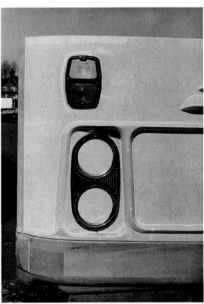

United and Northern General were keen rivals even after they both came into the National Bus Company. Northern took two batches of Bristol RE coaches: the first were service coaches with ECW bodies and the second, Plaxton bodied, for touring. The ECW vehicles were some of the most attractive in their short-lived NGT livery. These were to the shorter length and were subsequently down-seated to 45 as a result.

Left and below: Another piece of individuality was this 45-seater coach for Southern Vectis. This company had always taken a substantial number of lightweight coaches for its fleet and these tended to be to 'independent' specification. Thus XDL 122L had no driver's compartment as such (giving the impression that the driver was amongst the passengers), a non-Tilling moquette and illuminated side and rear fleet names. The door was manually operated.

Below left and centre: This type of step arrangement is commonly attributed to South Yorkshire PTE but of course first appeared on Brighton and Hove's Lodekkas in 1959/60. Strangely ECW was clearly examining it with NBC in 1973 as these two views show. Interestingly the windscreen on this buck was the flat form used up to 1972. It is a shame that NBC did not adopt it as this innovation would have been useful as an accessibility feature today. A very few non-NBC vehicles were built with it although some companies have retro fitted it.

The styling for the split step also showed another feature, below, which appears to have been a stillborn attempt to angle the original flat windscreens with a sharp 'Vee' form to the centre, rather like the LS bus – possibly to solve reflection problems., The only complete vehicles known to have anything remotely like this feature were the Sheffield Transport-ordered Fleetlines of 1974/5. However this photograph predates this batch even at the gestation stage in January 1973 and production adopted the BET screen shortly afterwards.

ECW adopted the BET screen across its range as the solution to the reflection problem. This was the Mark 2 VRT built in May 1973 for the then Department of the Environment – Transport has always been a Cinderella in Government and at this time did not even merit its own Ministry. A strange lack of attention to detail sees this official photograph taken without fitment of the offside fog light! NGP 226L seems to have been a brave bus as apart from working in the unit which today is the Driving Standards Agency, it led the return to Scotland for the type – now working for Rapsons/Highland Scottish in the far north at Wick.

United carried on with Bristol MWs in the BU class and in 1966. This was U725 (the B was dropped in 1964) and it shows the front which was unique to UAS build. Hardly the most elegant thing to be almost thrown onto an otherwise handsome body.

Bristol and thus ECW never really had a satisfactory small bus and United Counties small 1966 batch were no exceptions. Owing much to the MW, this was nonetheless an attractive bus, the more so because of the cream window rubbers. This batch had mixed lives, one being stored for two years prior to use – all were withdrawn after a mere four years.

Over the years ECW had an ambivalent attitude to refurbishment and accident repairs. Although some work was carried out it was not really geared to do this and the complex pay structure would not have helped an estimator in his endeavours. This was possibly a shame when the harsh 'eighties dawned. Two of the tasks which were undertaken are shown here. FMO 949, a Bristol LL, shows a neat conversion for one-man-operation. Although many operators undertook this type of work the edge clearly lay with the coachworks craftsmen as parts common to current production could be adapted. This Thames Valley vehicle was one of a couple which became pioneers in their own right when they passed to Tim Lewis's Continental Pioneer operation in Richmond and operated on service 235. This was virtually the first occasion that a London Transport service had been operated by an independent. How times have changed.

Far left: Another Coach Factory conversion for one-man-operation was of a Hants and Dorset LS in 1960. MLJ 146 was hardly the most attractive. The task was made difficult by a taper on the body and ECW seems to have taken the simplest (straight) line across the entrance, necessitating the peculiar tear drop shape afforded the quarter glass. For the record the draft deflectors at the top of the windscreens were present as this vehicle had *wind down* screens to comply with the then requirement for opening windscreens on PSVs.

Left: Compare the ECW effort with Crosville's in house variant which fits neatly across the entrance without creating the notch, leaves the quarter glass intact and also preserves the graceful curve of the waist moulding. On the other hand ECW had the edge on the Destination Box. This vehicle has the later split outward-opening screen.

Hants and Dorset had clearly learned the 'one-man' lesson for by 1964 it was taking all its coaches with express doors – not in fact an unattractive option. This vehicle, AEL 6B, is one which is rarely seen as it was destroyed, along with its twin AEL 7B.

The interior of this coach shows ECWs normal sumptuous coach seats. Comparison with United MW touring coach of 1962 above shows many similarities – glove nets, tables etc together with a somewhat safer grab strap. The effect of removing the quarter lights and replacing them with luggage racks can be seen. The effect is not unacceptable and net roller blinds were also proved. The only slightly jarring note perhaps is the full height partition behind the door.

Lowestoft Corporation whose garage was so near to the coach works was precluded from taking locally built bodies for many years. As soon as it was able however, this was righted and a small batch of AEC Swifts were taken. The town then remained loyal to the Coach Factory although its last order for VRTs was actually delivered to Eastern Counties after take-over.

And so this retrospect on one of Britain's best loved coachbuilders draws to a close – sadly like the Coach Factory itself. Everyone will have his or her personal favourite but let these two views of possibly the most famous product – the Lodekka – draw down the curtain.

2226 WW, a 60-seat rear entrance vehicle of 1960 for York West Yorkshire (YDX 92), shows just a hint of modernity with fluorescent lighting and offside illuminated advertisement panel. Somewhat surprisingly it wears Midland General destination blinds for Clay Cross – the view was certainly taken by ECW's official photographer of the time, Lawrence Gall.
5101 HN was a slightly later but extremely rare FSF 60-seater – with cream window gasket. BL 101 was, quite appropriately, for the United fleet, long since departed as the owner of the Coach Factory, but nonetheless an important customer to the end.

"We SHALL remember them"